THE BIRTH OF DEATH AND OTHER COMEDIES

OTHER WORKS BY TOM WHALEN

Elongated Figures

The Camel's Back (with Michael Presti)

Roithamer's Universe

A Newcomer's Guide to the Afterlife: On the Other Side Known Commonly As "The Little Book" (with Daniel Quinn)

Winter Coat

Dolls: Prose Poems

THE BIRTH OF DEATH AND OTHER COMEDIES
THE NOVELS OF RUSSELL H. GREENAN

BY TOM WHALEN

DALKEY ARCHIVE PRESS
CHAMPAIGN • DUBLIN • LONDON

First edition, 2011

Library of Congress Cataloging-in-Publication Data

Whalen, Tom.
The birth of death and other comedies : the novels of Russell H. Greenan / Tom Whalen. -- 1st ed.
p. cm.
Includes bibliographical references.
ISBN 978-1-56478-640-1 (pbk. : alk. paper)
1. Greenan, Russell H.--Criticism and interpretation. I. Title. II. Title: Novels of Russell H. Greenan.
PS3557.R376Z97 2011
813'.54--dc22
2011010757

Partially funded by a grant from the Illinois Arts Council, a state agency, and by the University of Illinois at Urbana-Champaign

www.dalkeyarchive.com

Cover: design and composition by Danielle Dutton, photo of Russell H. Greenan by Andy Browder
Printed on permanent/durable acid-free paper and bound in the United States of America

For Annette
and all the students who enjoyed Greenan along with me

CONTENTS

PREFACE
9

INTRODUCTION
"It's No Joke":
The Dark Fiction of Russell H. Greenan
11

CHAPTER ONE
The Mechanical Universe
of *Nightmare* (1970)
31

CHAPTER TWO
Realism and Allegory in
The Queen of America (1972)
41

CHAPTER THREE
"Alone in the Void":
The Secret Life of Algernon Pendleton (1973)
51

CHAPTER FOUR
"A Myriad of Disquieting Considerations":
Heart of Gold (1975)
65

CHAPTER FIVE
The Devil to Pay in the Paradigm:
The Bric-a-Brac Man (1976)
81

CHAPTER SIX
"A Pretty Gloomy Idea":
The Trickster Figure in *Keepers* (1978)
98

CHAPTER SEVEN
A Bucket of Maggots, *A Can of Worms* (1987):
Methods of Order in Greenan's Macabre Collage
111

CHAPTER EIGHT
"What an Edifice of Artifice!":
It Happened in Boston? (1968)
126

CODA:
Reflections on the Literary Career
of Russell H. Greenan
166

BIBLIOGRAPHY
178

PREFACE

For three decades word of mouth has kept alive Greenan's brilliant first novel *It Happened in Boston?* Back in print as a Modern Library 20th Century Rediscovery, *It Happened in Boston?* is one of the most fascinating novels to appear in the 1960s, and is being rediscovered by a new generation of readers. Few, however, are aware of the seven novels that followed *It Happened in Boston?* between 1970 and 1987.

Since *It Happened in Boston?* is Greenan's best-known novel and within it can be found most of his characteristic themes and techniques, I use it as a touchstone to analyze his other novels, beginning, after an introductory chapter, with his second, *Nightmare*, and proceeding in order of appearance to *A Can of Worms*, before treating *Boston?* more fully. No English-language editions exist to date of the two novels published in France, *La nuit du jugement dernier/Doomsnight* and *Magique micmac/Glamour Doom*. His latest novel, *Dread of Night*, appeared after my work was completed. These three novels are not, therefore, discussed in depth, but are mentioned briefly, especially in the coda that looks at the reception of Greenan's books and reflects on his career.

I would like to thank Althea Greenan for her good work on behalf of her father's books, Russell H. Greenan who allowed me to quote from his letters to me, Wolfgang Hochbruck and David Vancil for their advice and encouragement, Paul Rosheim of Obscure Publications who brought out the chapter on *It Happened in Boston?* as a limited-edition chapbook, James Barszcz of *College Hill Review* where the chapter on *A Can of Worms* first appeared, and Annette Wiesner for her long-lasting support of this project.

The chapters which follow are not meant in any sense as definitive readings of the dark comedies of this criminally neglected American master, but only as suggestive glimpses into the universe of his books, and as an homage, of course, and justification for a reader's obsession.

22 December 2009

INTRODUCTION

"IT'S NO JOKE": THE DARK FICTION OF RUSSELL H. GREENAN

In the late seventies and early eighties I often dreamed that a new novel by Russell H. Greenan (1925–) had become available, printed and present in whatever phantasmal bookstore I had entered. Sometimes I knew their plots; sometimes I read in sharp dreamscript a few sentences. What delight I felt knowing soon I would be able to immerse myself in another dark, original work by Greenan, and how disappointed I was when the novel in hand dispersed on waking.

My dreaming Greenan novels wasn't due to a young man's predilection for a particular genre. Which one would that be anyway? Not horror, though Greenan's second novel, *Nightmare* (1970), and third, *The Queen of America* (1972), were marketed by Random House as "A Contemporary Tale of Horror" and "A Horror Story," respectively. (Random House published the first six of Greenan's novels, as well as the 2003 reissue of his first novel *It Happened in Boston?* as a Modern Library 20th Century Rediscovery.) One can almost sympathize with the publisher's difficulties in marketing his books. His fifth novel, *Heart of Gold* (1975), where Christian issues and references collide with the confidence game to produce a complex and rather stern masterpiece of black humor, was labeled "A Melodrama" and his sixth, *The Bric-a-Brac Man* (1976), "An Extravaganza." For his fourth novel, *The Secret Life of Algernon Pendleton* (1973), Random House understandably had no tag, though a blurb by Ira Levin tells us on the cover that Greenan is "a one-of-a-kind writer" and the novel "*endearing*." The cover of his first novel *It Happened in Boston?* (1968) calls it—simply, accurately—"an extraordinary novel." Yes, all his novels are that.

Crime fiction, then? Yes, in that crimes occur, especially murders, though his novels shed this genre's conventions faster than the best of them: Hammett, say, or Cain, Goodis, Bardin, Thompson, Highsmith, or Himes. As different as these authors are, and they are very different, Greenan's novels in any list of noir authors stand out. The same holds if we try to enroll his work in the army of horror, though it's true that he descends from the romance tradition of Hawthorne and Poe, where allegory and dream mingle with and illuminate realism. Greenan's books, as Christopher Lehmann-Haupt said in his *New York Times* review of *The Bric-a-Brac Man*, "are difficult to classify, therefore hard to explain." In the "Afterword" to the new edition of *It Happened in Boston?* Greenan states that he "would not have been surprised if it had failed to find a publisher. Editors like to categorize things—a very human trait—and my offbeat tale did not fit easily into any ordinary classification" (2003, 281).

Perhaps Poe's term Arabesque is the one to affix to Greenan's work. "What characterizes the Arabesques," says Daniel Hoffman in *Poe Poe Poe Poe Poe Poe Poe*, "is their exploration of extreme psychological states—the narrators or chief characters are often madmen, or persons who undergo some excruciating suffering of the soul" (206). Poe's lines from "The Conqueror Worm"—"And much of Madness, and more of Sin, / And Horror the soul of the plot" (Poe, *Complete* 961)—apply to Greenan's books, but so do they to works by Dostoyevsky, Faulkner, and Flannery O'Connor. Hoffman also says that "[c]hief among [Poe's] themes is duplicity itself. The doubleness of experience" (206)—represented in *It Happened in Boston?* in the artist/God doubling; in *The Secret Life of Algernon Pendleton* in Eulalia, a porcelain pitcher that serves as the narrator's alter ego; and in *The Bric-a-Brac Man* in a look-alike cousin whose identity the narrator takes over. This doubleness dialectically rises whenever a mad character's duplicitous point of view dominates, as it frequently does in Greenan's work.[1]

Perhaps, though, as with other out-of-genre authors to whom Greenan's work may be compared—Hawthorne, Gogol, Poe, Kafka, West, and Nabokov come readily to mind—we might as well call the books after the author's name rather than this or that genre. What, then, is a Greenan? Greenans are grotesque, gleeful, comic, grim. Bad puns mingle with high allusion, death lies down with deception, money rattles then strangles the soul, eccentricity merges with madness. Murders abound, stylish Grand Guignol ones. Buildings are derived from but never imitate the labyrinthine constructions of Gothic romances and are peopled with comic and not-so-comic grotesques. Elaborate traps are set (by what? by whom? a universal malignity? a vengeful god?) and few escape the trap's snap at the end, or if so only metaphysically, a dubious kind of escape. Greed and money drive the plots. "Money and murder aren't exactly strangers to each other in this world," says a character in *The Bric-a-Brac Man* (198). And all of it written in a style somewhere between the baroque and the minimalist, filled with

1 I will address again the difficulty of categorizing Greenan's fiction and the effect this difficulty has had on his career in my coda.

erudition (and erudite madmen) especially about art, various killing techniques, the antique trade (Greenan himself was a dealer for a time and his subjects are meticulously researched)—a style willing to brave vaudevillian turns on the one hand (more than one comedian pratfalls to his death) and Nabokovian anagrams on the other (Rengane, Enganar, Sursell, the "clever Le Sur"(*It Happened in Boston?* 10).

Always the details are as clean as a scalpel. "A drop of rain touched my cheek as I strode with casual speed out to Charles Street. Another tapped my hat as I bounded across Beacon Street" (*It Happened in Boston?* 270). It's happening in Boston, all right. His books are filled with a precise realism—a boy's hand opens like "a somewhat grimy flower" (*It Happened in Boston?* 13); an avaricious old man's "mauve nether lip [is] aquiver" (*Heart of Gold* 51–52)—that form "a matrix of details so densely textured as to make the improbable seem solidly believable," as Anne Tyler noted in her 1982 reappraisal of *It Happened in Boston?* Often, too, they are charged with the hallucinatory clarity of a paranoiac's Weltanschauung: "It was the philodendrons, I guess, that jolted me out of my languor. They nagged me relentlessly, whispering and muttering the same old accusation . . . After a few days one of the plants—a tangled, dense, dusky-green specimen in a majolica jardiniere—began to shout so loudly that wherever I retreated to in the house, I could still hear his vile taunts and insults" (*The Secret Life of Algernon Pendleton* 191).

Greenan's characters are isolated by, variously, their madness, special talents, and eccentricities, that is, their inner beings.

> Each man lives his life in a manner peculiar to himself alone. Even the most well-oiled, precisely machined cog in the complex gear-train of modern society—and I am

> not one of these, much as I crave order—has within himself a unique core that distinguishes him from those about him. This inner being exists only for itself and is forever at war with the inner beings of others. (*It Happened in Boston?* 8)

The "I" of *It Happened in Boston?* or Alfred Omega, as he calls himself at one point, has the hypersensitivity of one of Poe's comic madmen who are also "forever at war with the inner beings of others." "Sometimes I try to hear the sunlight or to imagine colors not derived from the primaries or to visualize the universe with all the space removed" (11). Alfred Omega aspires to unseat God and will murder seven people for the chance. At times this madman is as charming as Xavier de Maistre writing about his voyage and nocturnal expedition around his room (*Voyage Around My Room* [1794]; *Nocturnal Expedition Around My Room* [1825]), except Greenan's murderer prefers to spend his time beneath his bed.

> Truly, I believe that to be under a bed is the nearest man can come to paradise here on earth. That cozy space is a room within a room, a world within a world. It is a magic mantle of invisibility, a catacomb, a secret chamber in the haunted house of society. Who knows? In the end it may well be the last refuge of humanity. How wise, then, is man to bring into his home, in the center of a sprawling metropolis, one small bush from the jungle! If, as Plato avers, there is a perfect bed in heaven, then I am sure that God spends a good part of His time beneath it. (80)

Greenan's protagonists madly totter atop a mountain of misfortune, malfeasance, and murder, then tumble at the end deeper into madness or into death or metaphysics. To the American pantheon of comic masterpieces narrated by madmen—Poe's "The Tell-Tale Heart," "The Black Cat," The Fall of the House of Usher"; Fitz-James O'Brien's "The Diamond Lens"; Thompson's *The Killer Inside Me, Pop. 1280*; Nabokov's *Despair, Lolita, Pale Fire*—should be added *It Happened in Boston?* and *The Secret Life of Algernon Pendleton*—a limited pantheon and a difficult subgenre to artistically embody. Of these two novels and the others by Greenan—readers, beware. The flame fascinates but may mesmerize the naïve. We laugh at the pratfalls and puns, revel in his Grand Guignol murders, delight in his wit and artistry, and some of us even dream non-existent Greenans. But like Melville's unseeing Captain Delano aboard the San Dominick, we walk on ground "every inch . . . mined into honey-combs" (*The Piazza Tales* 115).

At some point in the Greenan game, one feels caught in a whirl of connections—the world is "charged with many unsuspected possibilities and potentialities" (*The Secret Life of Algernon Pendleton* 99). Speculative paths, metaphysical and theological, spin dizzyingly out from his narrative seeds. A man believes he can meet God and kill Him. Another believes he can send gold to himself in the afterlife. Another that nothing ever dies, so it's all right to shoot his depressed best friend in the head. Again and again Greenan's plots reach a point where the protagonist steps back and catalogues the knots in the rope tightening around his neck and wonders if his world is real. "Was I living in the real world or had I plunged into some psychotic delusion?" (*The Bric-a-Brac Man*

192). "In Whitey Frainer's life fantasy and reality often became confused. Seeing this odd scene below him, he wondered if he was dreaming" (*A Can of Worms* [1987] 52).

In *The Power of Blackness,* Harry Levin points out that Poe's preference was "to dwell in the psychology of crime," the *act* of the madman and the effect of his act on himself, whereas Hawthorne's concern was with "the ethics of guilt" (146). Greenan combines these two strands in his "crime" stories. His plots and characters may perform Poe-like pirouettes, but a moral concern more akin to Hawthorne also drives them, though the direction of Hawthorne's nineteenth- and seventeenth-century Bostonians is, according to Milton R. Stern, toward "damnation and redemption" (Hawthorne, *The House of the Seven Gables,* xxii), whereas Greenan's twentieth-century world is more austere, with his characters moving primarily toward damnation. "Then it ended. It was all over—and in this world, Lenox suffered no more" (*Heart of Gold* 276).

Greenan, like Hawthorne, flirts with but never embraces allegory. Here's the Devil in the disguise of an insurance salesman (or maybe the narrator only thinks Mr. Beels is Beelzebub) in *It Happened in Boston?*:

> "I am not an American, Mr. Barber. You are quite right. Still, I have a little American blood in me," he declared, while a twisted smile formed on his thin lips as if to imply that he had only just quaffed a tumbler of that precious fluid. "I am of mixed ancestry: my forebears were a polyglot group and I, the last of the line, have an easy familiarity with a host of languages. Frontiers mean little to me, sir. I have associates in every nation, many in positions

> of great influence. I have business affiliations—not merely in the assurance field but in securities, real estate and banking—in every corner of the globe." (24)

And here the Devil is (in the disguise of a Mexican madman—well, he claims Mexico as his "adopted" country) in *The Bric-a-Brac Man*:

> "Let Him up there receive the atheists and agnostics," he stated, directing his dark, cocker-spaniel eyes toward the ceiling. "In heaven there are plenty of vacancies. It is virtually empty, that place. Also, a nonbeliever is not a genuine sinner. How can you sin if you have no creed? How can you be faithless if you profess no faith? How can you be an outlaw if you are convinced that the universe is devoid of laws?" (76)

These two devils wouldn't be as devilish if reduced to mere allegory. "All that would be much too like a Gothic romance," says the narrator of *It Happened in Boston?* "I suspect a deeper and far more interesting meaning" (212).

Greenan does, however, as in the case of Mr. Beels above, take advantage of allegorically flavored names. In Hawthorne we encounter, among many others, Goodman, Faith, Dimmesdale, and Portsoaken; equally welded to his name is Steven Pierglass, the narrator of *Nightmare*. Pierglass works for a voice named John that has hired him to move into a mostly black tenement house in New York City and identify the black blackmailer of a national politician and murderer, John's mysterious client. "This place is like the House of Usher—dreary and eerie," says one of the tenants (72). Pierglass, who like many of Greenan's characters, shifts on the scale from sympathetic human to sociopath, is, as his name might imply, epistemologically challenged—as are we all—and *Nightmare*, in turn, an experiment in point of view.

As tightly as Kafka closes in on his K. and Josef K. (originally an "I" Kafka later turned into a "he"), Greenan locks us into the narrow perspective of Pierglass. We see only what he sees. "Twisting my neck, I peered upward" (7). (The reflexive pun is hardly a random act, as few things are in Greenan's fictional universes.) "I tried to get a better look at her through the plexiglass" (22). The correlate for Pierglass's entrapment and his final executioner is the G.A.B.A. (Gravity Actuated Ball Automaton)—"It's a machine. Would you like to see it?" its designer asks Pierglass (17). "I looked, blinked, and looked again. The room was long but not very wide, and from one end to the other it was laced with plastic tubing. It was like a nest of transparent serpents. Tie rods and stanchions, brackets and cables held the various sections in place, as the thing meandered with many loops and detours in every direction" (17). As blinkered as Oedipus, Pierglass sees the room but doesn't perceive that it's a *mise en abîme* into which he will fall at the novel's end. Caught in his own reflexive gaze, he's a mechanical doll lost in a dollhouse of mirrors. "It seemed to me that I'd forgotten nothing" (16). But of course, as it turns out, he has and what he's forgotten will cost him his life.

The ending of Greenan's first novel suggests another link to Hawthorne, his use of a "formula of alternative possibilities," in Yvor Winters's phrase (170). In *It Happened in Boston?* are we reading, for example, the classic mythic pattern of the death and rebirth of the hero or the final death-vision (sent to us from the other side?) of a madman? Has he really succeeded in killing

God and being crowned the new King or is he adrift in one of his many reveries? The possibilities proliferate. When I used to teach *It Happened in Boston?* (for three decades using battered copies of the hardback editions and tattered, rubber-banded copies of the Fawcett paperback), my final test question was open-book: "In your opinion, what happens to the narrator at the end? What is his fate? Justify your theory with textual evidence." In an interview with Modern Library to promote the new edition of *It Happened in Boston?,* when asked whether he thought the novel's "haunting, ambiguous ending" was "a dark ending to a dark tale, or a happy ending to a sad tale," Greenan responded that for him "it's both. I felt that, given the other ambiguities in the novel, the ending had to be open to more than one interpretation. The ending, like the story itself, means what the reader thinks it means." Jonathan Lethem, in his introduction to the new edition says, "I reach a different conclusion each time I read the book" (xi).

Central to American literature and some of the dark comedies of Melville, Twain, West, Faulkner, Thompson, and Greenan is the confidence man or trickster figure. The characters who resemble or claim to be the Devil in *It Happened in Boston?* and *The Bric-a-Brac Man* are confidence men of a sort, and so is God, at least according to the unnamed narrator of *It Happened in Boston?* (or multi-named, he gives himself several names in the novel, from Alfred Omega to Mr. Totality). So are other Greenan characters, including the protagonists of *Nightmare* and *Heart of Gold,* in that they thrive on and die in a state of deception.

The trickster figure and psychopathic killer in *Keepers* (1978), Nigel Vaughan, is also that bleak novel's least deluded character. Nigel lacks the appeal of Algernon Pendleton, with his talking ceramic pitcher and head injury in the war as an excuse for his madness, but with his puns and quotes and esoteric knowledge and, in the context of the Greenan universe, a justifiable misanthropy ("I discovered it's a rather ghastly place, the world" [14]), he is not without his own charm.

> "Faced with prolonged misery and certain death, the so-called normal man has a desperate need of tricks and stratagems if he wishes to go on living," said Nigel, as he cut his fingernails with a clipper. "Confronted with the stark horror of reality, the sane person requires all manner of illusions—defense mechanisms, they're aptly termed—in order to survive, for without these self-deceptions he would have motivation for nothing but suicide."
>
> "A pretty gloomy idea," Osgood commented indifferently.
>
> "I'll say it is—yet true nonetheless. I helped a man commit suicide at Rose Hill Manor, years ago. Showed him how to tear his shirtsleeves off and twist them into a noose. There was a great furor when they found him hanging from a pipe in the bathroom. They cut him down in such haste that his body landed on the washbasin and tore it off the wall. There was water everywhere. A Frenchman once killed himself with a grand piano. He hoisted it up to the ceiling with ropes and pulleys, made himself comfortable underneath it, and then cut the thing

loose. It must have flattened him into a crêpe suzette, eh? A bizarre race, the French. Gérard de Nerval, a fine poet, used to drink his wine from a human skull. He claimed it was his mother's, and that he had to kill her to get it. Ha, ha! What I'm saying, Edward, is that normal people aren't as sure-sighted as they believe—that the images registering on their brains are not the same as those their eyes beheld initially. As Edgar Allan Poe observed,

> '*All that we see or seem,*
> *Is but a dream within a dream.*'

So when psychiatrists contend that madmen lose touch with reality, the good doctors are deluding themselves. It's the sane who dwell in a fantasy world, and the insane who see things as they actually are. That's why they go crazy." (58–59)

In the character of Nigel Vaughan, Greenan has combined two of his character types, the psychotic and the jokester. Nigel's punning links him to other Greenan jokesters (Mary Urquhart, for example, from *Heart of Gold*; Pendleton's great-grandfather in *The Secret Life of Algernon Pendleton*; the narrator of *It Happened in Boston?*) and the old vaudevillians and comedians (Manny Portobello in *Nightmare*, Leo Slocum in *The Bric-a-Brac Man*) whose stale jokes sometimes lend a sense of failure more than levity to the enterprise of life. Nigel's jokes, because they come from a madman and manipulator, are trickier to judge.

"I'll bet you don't even know when arias are supposed to be sung—do you, Edward?"

"Arias? Is it some kind of riddle? I give up, if it is."

> With his oddly shaped hand, Nigel patted the coarse black hair on the crown of his head, and replied triumphantly, "Arias must be sung at opera-tune moments. Ha, ha!" (13–14)

In part the jokes are meant to be disarming. Listen. I'm only a madman. Harmless. A murderer, yes, possessing great physical strength, but with a mind filled with trivia. A child, you see, all in all. Harmless as a child. Won't you help me? Another joke: Does his listener know where Noah kept the bees? No. "In the archives. Ha, ha! That's quite funny, isn't it?" To which his listener replies, "Yes—a real knee-slapper. Where do you get them all?" (131). And sometimes the jokes are meant to needle and terrify and, perhaps, expose a truth. Discussing in detail his knowledge, both historical and personal, of cannibalism with Edward Osgood, the young man hired by Nigel's politician brother to watch over his mad sibling, "[t]he lunatic regarded his listener benignly, waiting for him to comment on the anecdote, but Osgood appeared so flabbergasted by what he had heard that he could offer nothing at all" (150–51). When he finally elicits a response of "That's sick" from Osgood, Nigel says,

> "I'm reminded of a joke. Some cannibals caught a missionary, and one of them said to the chef, 'Are you going to broil him?' And the chef answered, 'No, he's a friar.' Ha, ha! Don't you think that hilarious, my boy?"
>
> "No. I'm still thinking about those Fiji Islanders. They must have been worse than wild animals."
>
> "Of course they were. They were human beings," Nigel replied, grinning. (151–52)

"He's kind of comical, isn't he?" Osgood asks his boss's personal secretary, who replies, "In a macabre sort of way" (19).

"It is our world in the process of becoming our hell," as R. W. B. Lewis accurately described Melville's *The Confidence-Man: His Masquerade* (267). Greenan's worlds, too, follow a similar direction as his characters dupe and are duped, cheat and are cheated, until the deceit that ensnares them comes grotesquely, macabrely, comically clear.

> Suddenly all is clear. The filthy wretches! . . . Victor is nothing but a swindler, a confidence trickster . . . He has woven a web of such intricacy that I cannot see the beginning or even imagine the end, but I am truly snared in its glittering filaments. What fantastic knavery . . .
>
> I have gone completely insane, I thought . . .
>
> This English, this British brigand, has passed off my picture as an original Leonardo! (*It Happened in Boston?* 232)

The theme of the confidence game in American literature often serves the purpose of satire. Especially in novels like *Nightmare*, originally titled and published in the United Kingdom as *Nightmare in Colour* (1971), an incisive look at race relations in the late 1960s; *The Queen of America*, on one level a critique of American capitalism; and later work like *A Can of Worms*, *La nuit du jugement dernier/Doomsnight* (1990), and *Dread of Night* (2009), where small-crook schemes mingle with larger political ones, Greenan focuses his satirical eye on a distinctly American brand of *Homo Corruptibilus*. Like Mark Twain, he presents a world where woodyards will always be "piled by them cheats so you can throw a dog through it anywheres" (Twain 158).

In *The Adventures of Huckleberry Finn* Huck explains to Aunt Sally that his return was delayed because "We blowed out a cylinder-head." "Good gracious!" says Aunt Sally, "anybody hurt?" "No'm. Killed a nigger," says Huck (280). Racism is the object of Twain's satire, social class Evelyn Waugh's in the comparable opening of *A Handful of Dust*:

> "Was anyone hurt?"
>
> "No one, I am thankful to say," said Mrs. Beaver, "except two housemaids who lost their heads and jumped through a glass roof into the paved court. They were in no danger. The fire never reached the bedrooms, I am afraid. Still, they are bound to need doing up, everything black with smoke and drenched in water and luckily they had that old-fashioned sort of extinguisher that ruins everything. One really cannot complain. The chief rooms were completely gutted and everything was insured. Sylvia Newport knows the people. I must get on to them this morning before that ghoul Mrs. Shutter snaps them up." (7)

The indifference of Waugh's and Twain's characters to death serves the purpose of social commentary. When Greenan's characters behave in a similar manner, the critique goes to something equally or even more elemental in the human condition. In *The Bric-a-Brac Man* the sisters Lydia Crabtree and Elvira Lambert are discussing the death of the former's husband with Arnold Hopkins, the novel's eponymous figure, who besides dealing in antiques is a confidence man (in this scene he's taken the name of another dealer, Guilfoyle) and thief.

> "When Michael's head hit the sidewalk it burst open like an overripe beefsteak tomato," said the widow with apparent satisfaction. "That's how hard he came down. I couldn't recognize him, Mr. Guilfoyle, and we'd been married twenty-six years. Fell headfirst, he did. You could actually see his brains on the sidewalk."
>
> "You could see his brains," murmured the doll-faced Lydia as she offered me a plate of macaroons.
>
> "Life is tragic," I remarked, taking a cookie. (82)

In conversation with her pastor, the ethically challenged Rev. Lenox from *Heart of Gold*, an old Boston socialite describes a dead usurer as an "odious creature. His whole character was permeated with greed. Toward the end of his life he came to look like a mask of the devil. Really! He was the final distillation of the venom of usury." To which Reverend Lenox replies, "Nicely put, my dear. Are these ladyfingers?" (33). After withdrawing "the blood-drenched weapon from the dying Pomerantz" (a private detective, blackmailer, and former school chum of his killer), Stanley Gloag of *A Can of Worms* looks out of the window of the car, and "saw two well-dressed men approaching on foot from the direction of Copley Square, advancing at a leisurely pace and conversing in a cadent undertone."

> Gloag froze, holding the dripping knife between his legs to keep the blood off his clothing. His face was empty, but his cowled eyes gleamed like embers in the darkness.
>
> The interlopers drew near. He could see them quite distinctly—one in a gray topcoat with the collar up, the other in a fashionable suede jacket.

> ". . . how she ever keeps that beautiful figure, because she eats like a pig," the closer of the two was saying in a clear crisp voice. "I took her to the DuBarry over on Newbury Street and the bill came to ninety-seven dollars. She ate everything but the tablecloth, and guzzled a whole bottle of sparkling Burgundy. The girl must've fasted for a week before that meal, but I still don't know . . ."
>
> The words faded as the strollers, having passed the parked Omni without so much as a casual glance at it, moved farther away.
>
> "Thank God for the tinted windows," Stanley whispered as he wiped his switchblade clean on Frederick Pomerantz's flannel trousers. (158)

Food and death. Greed, gluttony, and death. And an indifference to the life and death of others flavored with a stringent sociopathology.

Stanley Gloag: a Boston punk, a hired killer, one of many characters in *A Can of Worms* caught in a sex-, deceit-, and greed-driven plot. He might have popped out of a mixture of Flannery O'Connor's Misfit ("A Good Man Is Hard to Find") and Jim Thomspon's Carl Bigelow (*Savage Night*). This wiry little sadist responds to Pomerantz's asking where the conflict of interest is in the contract he wants Stanley to fulfill and the as-yet-unspecified one Stanley has already accepted, with:

> "Well . . ." Gloag let the enigmatic syllable hang unsupported in the close warm air of the automobile for several seconds, before adding, "the thing is complicated."

> "Sounds simple enough to me. Just a matter of priority, ain't it? I don't want to be inquisitive, Stan, but is this other guy you have to scrag somebody I know or what?"
>
> "You know him, yeah. Funny coincidence, isn't it? The other murder contract is on you, Fritzie. So after I hit you, who's going to pay me for hitting the big dinge?"
>
> The investigator's mouth jerked open. For a moment he stared at Gloag in disbelief, then he grinned and said, "Stanley, you got a weird sense of humor. But you always did, even back in the old days. A contract on *me*, for crying out loud. That's a good one. No more jokes, though, huh? I'm very serious about this thing."
>
> "So am I," said the man in the cap. "It's no joke. I was going to go looking for you tomorrow, then you called me up and saved me some trouble." (153)

Gloag tells Fritz he "must've made a mistake somewhere along the line" (154), as if he were speaking to the grandmother O'Connor's Misfit is about to dispatch, though unlike the Misfit, Stanley Gloag just might be a believer. "Thank God for the tinted windows," Stanley says, and when he dies he appears to the policeman who has killed him "as if [he] were making the sign of the cross" (174). How could Fritz have gotten "mixed up in a grift like this," Stanley asks, then offers Pomerantz the chance "to recite a quick Our Father" (156). Fritz wails that they've known each other for thirty years, that they watched *Pinocchio* together at the old University Theater, to which Gloag responds, "Hey, snap out of it. Thirty years got nothing to do with this. You trying to con me?" (156).

In Greenan's carnivalesques, riddled with greed, madness, confidence men, and murder, we look in vain for someone who isn't being conned or trying to con us. "The Prince of Condom" is what Mary Urquhart from *A Heart of Gold* calls her first lover, a "conscienceless con man" with a mouth "full of deceit and falsehoods" (139), and Mary herself is a master scam artist with a talent for composing letters of request for financial aid.

Comic and often deadly, the con games in Greenan's books proliferate, become universal, cosmic. In a dream of the swamp where his employer buries his victims, Steven Pierglass, the narrator of *Nightmare*, has his "eyes . . . drawn to the sky, but there was no sky—only a total blackness, like a gaping, bottomless hole in the universe" (170). Topsy-turvy, with the sky at the bottom, Pierglass's dream-vision is as black as Melville's "button-like black bubble" (*Moby-Dick* 625).

After the dream, Pierglass goes to the window and sees the moon "low in the western sky, like a lopsided smile on an invisible face" (171).

Greenan's nasty little killer Stanley Gloag had it wrong. It's a joke after all. That lopsided smile low in the west suggests that something out there is laughing down at us.

CHAPTER ONE

THE MECHANICAL UNIVERSE OF *NIGHTMARE* (1970)

> "It's almost as if someone has thrown a switch and disconnected me."
>
> —*It Happened in Boston?* (253)

Originally titled, more aptly, *Nightmare in Color*, *Nightmare*, Russell H. Greenan's follow-up to his acclaimed first novel *It Happened in Boston?* is a tight, spare marvel of plot manipulations set in the racially charged sixties. Though Greenan relocates his fictional universe to New York City,[2] he brings in its wake a wealth of *Boston?*'s methods, character constellations, and themes, including comedy's favorite straight man, death. Yes, death is back, and so are murderers, metaphysicians, madmen, conspiracies, cats, and devious, off-screen machinations. This time though, the milieu isn't the art world of Boston, but a black tenement house. Hired to find the black blackmailer of a national politician (the blackmailer knows the politician once killed a black child), Steven Pierglass, the novel's narrator, is inserted by John, his boss whom Pierglass knows only as a voice, into a world he cannot understand,

2 Greenan's other novels, with the exception of *Keepers*, take place principally in Boston.

not necessarily because of his race, but because of his species. The race issue in this novel will be played in part for laughs, since the blackmailer, it turns out, is a white anthropologist tattooing himself to look black because he believes black is not only beautiful but sublime. That Greenan takes this volatile material and makes of it a dark comedy, is one of the novel's several achievements.[3]

The allegorically named and perceptually handicapped Steven Pierglass isn't as baroquely mad (or divinely inspired?) as *Boston?*'s "Alfred Omega," the time frame of *Nightmare* not as elaborate, the characterizations leaner, and no one reveries on park benches or under beds. But in *Nightmare* we find an ample display of Greenan eccentrics, innocents, and psychos. Also, Pierglass's dreams are almost as vivid as the ones in the first novel, and he steps into the plot's trap with eyes even more open and unseeing than Alfred Omega's. It's not easy to escape the name your author gives you, especially when the universe is as mechanical as the one Pierglass finds himself in.

As much as in any novel by Greenan, fate locks down on his main character with all the inevitability of the mill wheel gears in the final images of Carl Theodor Dreyer's film *Vampyr* (1932)—the gears grind, sifting the flour over the vampire's assistant, a village doctor, until whiteness suffocates him, and the gears come to a halt. The correlate for Pierglass's entrapment and his executioner is also a machine, the G.A.B.A. (Gravity Actuated Ball Automaton). Pierglass takes two looks (does a kind of double-take, as does the reader)

3 Noted as well by Sara Blackburn in her review of *Nightmare* for the *Washington Post Book World* (Dec. 12, 1970): "It should be added that, at a time when so many white writers are using the black struggle as a basis for pretentious, ill-conceived, and self-serving fiction, Mr. Greenan's perspective and taste make him a welcome exception." In 1971, the novel was published in England with its original title *Nightmare in Colour* back in place.

when he's shown into Room 6 (in chapter 5) and sees for the first time this bizarre invention. "I looked, blinked, and looked again. The room was long but not very wide, and from one end to the other it was laced with plastic tubing. It was like a nest of transparent serpents. Tie rods and stanchions, brackets and cables held the various sections in place, as the thing meandered with many loops and detours in every direction" (17).[4] This peculiar machine on the one hand looks like a fool's toy, an eccentric's harmless contraption, as messy and dysfunctional as the tenement house in which it resides. But as we shall see later, amidst its "loops and detours" the Gravity Actuated Ball Automaton possesses a deadly mechanical efficiency.

The designer of this device, its loops and detours mirroring the plot of this and other Greenan novels, is Axel Shadmeister, a Greenan eccentric worthy of Nathanael West.

> His growth of hair was fantastic. Dappled and wavy, it radiated from his skull in all directions. Clumps of it plunged from his forehead and draped his temples. It flooded his jaws, cascaded from his chin and overran his neck. It streamed from his ears and nostrils and hung like Spanish moss from his eyebrows. He resembled a stuffed doll made by a palsied toymaker. (8)

This former anthropology professor (he was kicked in the head by a cassowary), who wishes to turn himself black, believes that humans are "[m]ere fungi on a speck of dust called the earth . . . A cluster of insignificant spores, lost in the enormity of time and

---

4 Besides the novel itself, this room resembles the "bowel-spun cordage" of Doctor Portsoaken's spider-infested apartment in Hawthorne's unfinished *Septimius Felton*. See *The Elixir of Life Manuscripts*, 133.

space" (101–2). Shadmeister is the mad scientist of the mechanical universe that Pierglass unwittingly inhabits. "It's quite an idea—all mechanical" (17), Shadmeister says of one of his inventions. Holding up a ball bearing to our narrator at a party in the building, he tells Pierglass that "nothing [is] more perfect" (141). To Pierglass, "'[i]t looks like a roller-skate wheel."

> "True," he replied. "But doesn't it also look like an atom? The balls are like the electrons, you see. And looked at another way, it could be the solar system, with the planets spinning about the inner ring—which could represent the sun. Indeed, without being too fanciful, one might say that the entire galaxy is no more than an immense ball bearing, whirling endlessly through space on its own axis. A great helix made up of fiery balls . . ."
>
> I felt dizzy. Perhaps I went to sleep while he was talking and he took the hint and left. In any case, when I next looked at the chair beside me, it was empty. (142)

But what are we to make of such a vision? The G.A.B.A. with its nursery nonsense gaga/gabble sound, replicates the universe we live in, atoms wheeling about other wheeling atoms, as if we're caught in Poe's cosmology as described in *Eureka, A Prose Poem* (1848)—"The plots of God are perfect. The Universe is a plot of God" (165)—without Poe's ecstatic visions—"the final ingathering" (180), the "final agglomeration of all things" (182). For another, the G.A.B.A., the Gravity Actuated Ball Automaton, represents both what we are (gravity actuated automatons) and our fate (death).[5]

---

5 Apropos, Greenan worked in the early sixties "as a branch manager of a ball-bearing company" ("Afterword," *It Happened in Boston?* [1983] 279).

The occupants of Greenan's "House of Usher" tenement also participate, albeit unwittingly, in the novel's mechanistic theme, among them Manny Portobello, a songwriter (one of several troupers found in Greenan's novels left over from vaudeville), who loves to tell jokes and talk about the old days.

> "A bunch of us were at Jimmy Palomino's place one night and Jack Joe had us all going with his monkeyshines. The man was amazing. He must've known fifty ways of taking a pratfall. Anyway, that night it got a little quiet at one point, the way it does sometimes at parties, and all of a sudden Nobble hops up from the couch and does a nose dive. It was a thing of beauty. Pow! Down into the rug he goes. We went into hysterics, no kidding. Then he started to wiggle along the wall like a snake, and we were holding our sides. After that he rolled over a couple of times and his feet came up in the air and started to flap around, like he was a trained seal. We howled. I'll bet it was a good five minutes before we realized the poor man was having a heart attack. We carried him to a car, but he was dead by the time we got to Medical Center. He was some comic, Jack Joe. Everybody loved him."
>
> Jesus, I thought to myself. (115)

What appears to be a comedy routine is the moment before death. We pratfall our way through and out of life. Jokes are premised on juxtapositions, and the fissure formed between what is juxtaposed we fall into when we laugh, and if we laugh again, as we do in Greenan's novels, it is from within the abyss of the absurd. Seeing is believing, this anecdote shows, but between belief and truth lies a great divide.

The bad puns Greenan's characters and jokes incline toward are also a form of automatic reflexivity. Of an out-of-place footlocker in which a dead body will later be found, Pierglass says, "Since it's a footlocker, maybe it walked away" (133). Thelma, a beautiful black shoplifter, responding to a warning from the black cab driver George Washington about drinking too much, says:

> "Don't worry about me, Georgie. I'm not the optician's daughter."
>
> "Who was she, baby?"
>
> "You don't know her, George? Two glasses and she made a spectacle of herself."
>
> Washington roared and slapped his thigh. "That's real funny. You're a funny girl, Thelma." (135)

And soon to be a funny, dead girl. When Pierglass objects to John's having killed her, John tells him not to "get maudlin." "'But why are you making such a fuss? What does one person, more or less, matter? The earth is teeming with people—like maggots on a gob of rotten cheese. Who'll miss one little mulatto?' He gave a partly stifled laugh" (164).

"Every human being is an abyss," Büchner's Woyzeck told us, "it makes you giddy to look down" (qtd. in Hamburger 182). Greenan's eerily cold vision of man trapped in a web of circumstances far from benign is leavened by the pleasures of aesthetic cognition—the patterns, the plotting, the wit, the allusiveness. "This place is like the House of Usher—dreary and eerie," says Thelma (72), who, like most of the tenants in the building, needs money, and who is also willing (grave error) to blackmail the narrator. Earlier, Pierglass asks Thelma if she doesn't think the story about Sonny (a black child whose father, in the course of the novel, loses his job and is killed by the police) peeling an onion for the first time isn't funny. She answers:

> "Why?"
>
> "I don't know. I keep thinking about it."
>
> "You're cracking up," she declared bluntly.
>
> "No . . . it's that the onion is like . . . like a parable. It's like life. You keep peeling the skin off, looking for something. And in the end, you take that last layer away, and there's nothing there—nothing at all."
>
> She threw me a withering look. "Baby, if you're going symbolic, you'd better get on something more potent than that bourbon booze." (121)

Everything meshes, everything locks into place in *Nightmare*, and the characters lose what little control they have over their fates—if they have any control to lose. The mechanistic nature of his characters' lives even seeps into their thoughts, tropes and dreams. One of Pierglass's nightmares within *Nightmare* turns mechanized when a voice in his dream sounds "like the voice of a mechanical doll" (28). "That black-white thing somehow keeps popping into my mind," says George Washington, one of the novel's murder victims, as if he has no more control of his thoughts than he does his life (136). Even a brown cat named Ralph eats his owner's canary with "his jaws working mechanically" (166).[6]

---

6 We first encounter this brown cat—a cousin of Poe's black cat and *Boston?*'s Mitya, whom we observe, over the course of several pages, dying of strychnine poisoning—on the first page of *Nightmare*: "In a corner a sleek brown cat sat like a bronze Egyptian idol. A beam of sunlight cast a rod of gold across the animal's flank, causing the fur to glitter. It regarded me with

Pierglass's problem is that he can't see what's in front of him; he's a slave, so to speak, an automaton to his own name. "Twisting my neck, I peered upward" (7). "I tried to get a better look at her through the plexiglass" (22). The black man he's been seeking turns out not to be black after all. "'But Shadmeister's white,' I whispered. 'Isn't he?'" (192). Disappointed by his inability to complete his assignment, John tells him he's "been gullible . . . shortsighted and negligent. You've been stupid" (179).

At the end of *Nightmare*, as Pierglass helplessly watches the G.A.B.A. run the ball through its sequence that will detonate a bomb, the mechanical fuses with the personal. "The ball dropped into a small brass drum with a sharp ping. A ratchet chattered. Then a strange noise—like the sound of a boiling kettle—filled my ears. I realized suddenly that it was coming from my own throat" (205). We're nearing the abyss of the dying first-person narrator, an abyss few authors approach. Dickens's David Copperfield bows out romantically with: "Oh Agnes, Oh my soul, so may thy face be by me when I close my life indeed; so may I . . . still find thee near me, pointing upward!" (870). Poe's William Wilson, caught in subjectivity's hell, hears/says: "In me didst thou exist—and, in my death, see by this image, which is thine own, how utterly thou hast murdered thyself" (*Complete* 641). And Kid Collins, the narrator of Jim Thompson's *After Dark, My Sweet* (1955), gut-shot by the woman he loves, relates at the omega point of his story:

> Then I stopped.
>
> I just kind of stopped all over. (*After Dark, My Sweet* 131)

---

unblinking eyes" (3). Though not a jackal, this brown cat sits as implacable as Anubis, guarding the entrance to Greenan's gothic building.

Equally audacious, Greenan kills off his first-person narrator with his final word, but without the sentimental touch of having his narrator sacrifice himself out of love, the soft center of some *noir* works.[7]

> The steel sphere flashed around a bend, murmuring to itself. Down a slanting conduit it shot, and up and around a broad loop, and away through another turn it went.
>
> "Shadmeister!" I called, my knees quaking and my eyes bulging in my head. The room became fluid and unreal. I had a sensation of falling—falling an immense distance.
>
> The ball dropped into a small brass drum with a sharp ping. A ratchet chattered. Then a strange noise—like the sound of a boiling kettle—filled my ears. I realized suddenly that it was coming from my own throat.
>
> "Axel Shadmeister!" I screamed. "Come back!"
>
> The G.A.B.A. clinked and clanked. Down from the ceiling the tongs came, and taking hold, effortlessly lifted the telephone from its cradle. (205)

Who is the automaton—the steel ball that murmurs to itself, as it loops and glides along, or the G.A.B.A. itself, now activated to self-destruct? Or is it Pierglass who shouts, as if he could swing the fulcrum back his way, "Axel Shadmeister! . . . Come back!"? And isn't Axel Shadmeister as much a product of his name as Pierglass? *Axel* equals *axle*, of course, which once meant *axis*, and in *Shadmeister* one finds both *shadow master* and *S[c]hadmeister*,

7 The power of Thompson's ending can be found in part in the physicality of its sounds: nine monosyllabic words, then the trochaic "over", and in the repetition of "I" and "stopped"—Beckett's minimalism, in a sense, without the Beckett narrators' desire for continuance: "I can't go on, I'll go on" (*The Unnamable* 476).

harm master. Even the soul, if that kettle whistling in Pierglass's throat is the soul of a dying man, may be a rudimentary machine. What in *Nightmare* isn't an automaton, what, in its universe, isn't mechanistic?

When the G.A.B.A. "lift[s] the telephone from its cradle" (205), *Nightmare* ends simultaneously with the narrator's (earthly) end. Even more precisely it concludes on the birth/death axis of its final word—*cradle*. Exactly *where* the word rocks the narrator after that—heaven? hell? the Eternal Return?—Greenan's smart mechanism doesn't say.

CHAPTER TWO

REALISM AND ALLEGORY IN *THE QUEEN OF AMERICA* (1972)

Ignacio Never, the fourteen-year-old protagonist of Greenan's third novel, *The Queen of America* (1972), never makes it to the novel's end, but the novel's eponymous figure, one Elisabeth Beaker, aka Betsy March, a sixteen-year-old runaway who killed her sister in California and a few other acquaintances on her trek east across the country to Cambridge, Massachusetts, is still around, after slashing her way through Ignacio's loved ones—Sandra Jean, a furniture maker on whom Ig has a crush, and Ig's beloved dog Ripper. Ig's paranoid Spanish historian father Louis Never—with theft, plagiarism, and murder (not in that order) in his past—she doesn't kill, but at the end he's seeing "golden devils" and carted off to an asylum. Ig, however, our Queen slaughters.

Not that Betsy is without a certain charm. In fact, she's rather likable at times. When Ronald Mooney, a Harvard student and porno film director, puts his hand on her thigh at the Zero Inn Café,

> Betsy smiled, one end of her mouth higher than the other. Delicately she brought the cake fork down on the invading hand. Then, while gazing straight into her victim's eyes, she gradually applied pressure to it. The youth's

> florid face grew tense and his lips twitched, though he made no outcry. Mesmerized, Ig watched the tips of the prongs burrow into the flesh. Five or six seconds elapsed before the grinning girl withdrew the fork and casually lay it on the table. (79)

Ig's problems far exceed those of most of literature's adolescents. Holden and Huck have it easy compared to Ig, on his own in Cambridge with a suicidal father who refuses to leave his room or let anyone in, a blackmailer threatening to tell the police about the bank robbery Ig perpetrated, and a homicidal psychopath coming to kill him. But even so, Ig's conflict in a sense is closer to the metaphysical confrontation found in, say, *Don Quixote*, in that Ig longs for realism in a world that one might politely call malign, and thus prone to greed, madness, and murder (the Holy Trinity of the Greenan plot) which in turn spawn horror, allegory, Catholicism, and other realism-resistant viruses.

Ig's dad has not come out of his room in over six months, leaving Ig and Mrs. Gringle the housemaid to tend to the professor's demands, and no one but Ig's dog Ripper to look after Ig, who doesn't attend school and spends most of his time listening to the tapes of his neighbors across the way whom he has bugged. Once again Greenan plays a variation on the "terrible building" of Gothic fiction. The Labyrinth, formerly a thirty-room Victorian apartment house, now sliced and chopped into a hundred rooms,

> was an intriguing edifice. The rapacity of the realtor had overcome the original architecture decisively. Ordering a crew of carpenters and plasterers to make a given number of rooms of such and such a size, he swept all before

> him. Symmetry and proportion were routed; comfort and elegance were vanquished. The result was curious. There were rooms of every imaginable shape—triangles, lozenges, half-moons, hexagons, and even a few in the form of kidneys and hourglasses.
>
> This violent renovation had produced other strange phenomena as well. Fancy moldings ran off behind pasteboard partitions; ornate chandeliers ended up in corners; and a single radiator might be called upon to heat two disparate dwellings. In Ronald Mooney's bedroom, there were half a fireplace and two thirds of an open closet.
>
> Connecting these one-, two-, and three-room flats was a network of dog-legged corridors and crooked stairways that meandered wherever it pleased. Those familiar with the place had long since labeled it "the Labyrinth," and recounted fabulous tales of lost visitors and tenants who had disappeared mysteriously. (30–31)

But for Ig, this House of Usher isn't a place of fantasy or the grotesque, but instead an inroad to realism, an escape from the Gothic world that dominates his life with his father.

> Ig loved the Labyrinth. It was his hunting ground. Using his binoculars and his hidden microphones, he bagged an endless variety of incidents there. He was a boy of peculiar sensitivities, too—capable of enjoying sights and sounds that others would certainly have found so common as to be painfully banal. A student pecking away at a typewriter, a group of men playing cards, a child galloping a hobby-horse, the shape of a lamp, the angle of a

> bent leg, the patterns of light and shadow, the rhythms of human speech, snoring, running water, the noise of a vacuum cleaner—all this was interesting to him. In the minutiae of everyday living, he discovered something fascinating. (31)

Ig revels in the reality of these overheard lives, their actuality. "It's authentic. It's all true," he says (17). But Ig's realism is selective. He's not interested in Mooney's porno filmmaking. "It was cheap. I mean it wasn't artistic or . . . or profound. And you have to have a code of honor. That's what I think anyway" (41). Most of all he longs to make a movie, to see the lips move as they speak the words on his tapes, something he believes the viewing public wants as much as he.

> "Everybody would want to see an authentic, actual scene taken from another human being's life—everybody. It would all be true—the words, the movements, the looks on the people's faces—the whole, entire thing. Don't you see, Betsy? It'd be the first really live entertainment ever. No rehearsal, no script, no make-up—nothing! Why . . . why, even the man shooting the movie wouldn't know what was going to happen next. Even the people being filmed couldn't be sure of what they were going to do or say next. Naturalism—that's what they call it.
>
> "And people want that, I think. Ever see pictures in the papers of bank holdups taken by hidden cameras? Don't it give you a special thrill, knowing it's all real? Sure it does. Suppose you had an entire scene—some spectacular episode, say, like a man committing a murder. Wouldn't that

> be tremendously interesting? Psychologists and criminologists—they'd love to get a thing like that, I bet. But even ordinary stuff would be valuable, because it wouldn't be phony or make-believe. It'd be honest, genuine, real, natural. It'd be beautiful—right?" (43)

"Yes," says Ronald Mooney, conning Ig, after Ig has made a similar speech to him, "and I'm certain that the times are ripe for a new, unvarnished realism. This modern theatricalism—moribund stuff, all of it" (102–03). "Great, Ronald," Ig responds. "I mean, if you can make a picture about people the way they actually are, that would be terrific" (103).

But how are people really? And how can this fourteen-year-old survive in a world where the Queen of America, wrapped in her blood-soaked robe, trumps Ig's realism? He can't. Who could, after living through the following Grand Guignol scene?

> The chest contained slaughter. Torn and bloody limbs crowded its interior. Sandra Jean's head, the neck terminating in a stump of ragged tissue, looked up at him from a corner. With one eye open and the other closed, she might have been winking flirtatiously at him, except that her mouth wore a hideous, brutal sneer. Hanks of gore-clotted hair framed this terrible visage, adhering to the temples and jaws. A gold maple-leaf earring was just visible in the tangled strands.
>
> Only inches away, Betsy's blood-freckled face was nestled in the crook of a detached arm. Eyes closed, lips parted, she seemed almost to sleep. What he could make out of her body appeared to be in one piece, but so great

> was the carnage that it was impossible to be sure. Chunks of raw flesh, mottled organs, a portion of a ribcage, bone with the marrow exposed, bits of gristle—all were heaped into the small area. On a pile of viscera, a once-white blouse lay, its fabric stained a brilliant, glistening scarlet.
>
> If Ig had been frightened previously, he was thrust now into the final extremity of terror. The shiver that had seized his lips rapidly took possession of the rest of him. Vividly he imagined a creaking floorboard, but when he had forced himself to look over his shoulder, the room was as empty as before. Silence hung like a viscous, invisible vapor all about him. Turning back, he reached out for the lid with twitching fingers, intending to bring it down on the ghastly spectacle that its raising had revealed. As he did so, Betsy opened her green eyes.
>
> For what seemed like minutes, though scarcely a second transpired, his gaze was locked in hers while his outstretched arm hovered frozen in the air. Then, almost languidly, the girl raised herself and began to climb out. (47)

With "her clothing dripping horror" (48) and her bayonet raised, she stalks but does not catch Ig. Not yet.

Such stylistic tour-de-forces, like the death of the cat in *It Happened in Boston?* and other grizzly tableaux in his funhouse fictions, show Greenan at play ("the mind," said Ruskin describing the grotesque in *The Stones of Venice*, "under certain phases of excitement, *plays* with *terror*" [qtd. in McElroy 2]). But Greenan's form of play, no matter how precise and controlled and reflexive the prose, no matter how comic or surreal its juxtapositions, is never only for fun. "With one eye open and the other closed, she might have been winking flirtatiously at him, except that her mouth wore a hideous, brutal sneer." The death-grin masks nothing, it only darkens the horror of its surround.

Realism, at least Ig's kind, can't handle this reality. What can? Perhaps allegory, or at least the hint of allegory. Is the insurance salesman Mr. Beels in *It Happened in Boston?* really Beelzebub, are the three sisters in *The Bric-a-Brac Man* the three fates? In many ways, Betsy March-Beaker-Alcott is America. For one thing she is the ideal consumer ("the music and the commercials and everything go right through my head—zoom!") in that she relishes being culturally consumed. "They sure make cool things these days," she tells Ig.

> "Back home I had this pair of sunglasses that had a transistor right in the part that goes over your ear. My mother bought it for me. It had an earplug, and nobody else could hear it. I used to lie on the beach and look at the waves, and just listen and listen. And if I wanted to shut everything out, I'd turn the volume up as high as it would go, and let the music and the commercials and everything go right through my head—zoom! Sometimes I dreamed I was Queen of America, and people had to bow and curtsy when they talked to me." She giggled. "That seems like a long, long time ago now. I must've been a little goofy." (44)

Not only does Betsy co-opt American literature (Louisa May Alcott, her favorite author), but American history as well, or at least the history of our British ancestors. After Betsy is captured and put away for murder, she manages to send a letter to Ig:

> I got a job in the library here and my back is almost broken from carrying books. But it's better than working in the laundry or some of the other jobs. And I get to read. I just finished this cool book about Queen Elizabeth of England. I read it because we have the same name. It turns out she chopped off her cousin Mary's head. And her boyfriend the Earl of Essex—she gave him the ax too. I really grooved with that book. Of course they didn't do anything to her, because she was Queen. Me they stuck in this dumb Ciegaville mental hospital. You know what else? That Elizabeth had red hair!! I'll bet you a cup of coffee and two donuts we're related. Funny that they have a book like that in this rathole. And they don't have a thing by Louisa May Alcott. (116)

She signs off with, "Your former friend, *Betsy Beaker* (alias *Queen Elizabeth of America*)" and in her P.S. tells him the "*SWAK* on the envelope doesn't mean *SEALED WITH A KISS*. It stands for *STAB WITH A KNIFE!*" (117).

If Betsy is America, what is Ig? Fat Buddy, the drug dealer who will assist in Ig's ignominious fall, says he'll light a candle in church for Ig, whom he calls a "prince, a king, an emperor" (114). Earlier, after Ig has given him money, he had compared Ig to Christ: "'You're a prince, Ig. You're Jesus Christ . . . no crap.' He sidled away, an idiotic grin on his broad face" (88).

Everyone wants something of Ig, usually money, and Ig would gladly lend it to them. For a while he can because he robs a bank and sees to it that the crime is pinned on the murderess Betsy. But money, the root of all evil, takes its toll on Ig's innocence. Blackmailed by Mooney, Ig ends up responsible for Mooney's freezing to death. Down and down he goes, taking downers (meprobomate) and uppers (dexedrine) given to him by Fat Buddy. ("Drugs?" he says. "These are only like cough drops. They relieve the painful tickle. You're scared of everything, man" [165])—until for Ig it's "as if nothing really matters any more" (209).

The Queen of America, now calling herself Louisa Mae, is last seen by another runaway on a "red Kawasaki Bushmaster. I think she said she was headed out West, actually" (214). The Queen of America lights out for her past, the Territory Ahead now also the Territory Behind, the violence of America its past and its future.[8]

Longing for authenticity (naturalism, realism), Ig is trapped between the "inauthentic" distorted desires of the mad Betsy and his mad father, and all around him consumerism and greed continue to grind away at the real. Even as he dies, his dream of authenticity plays on:

> "*. . . the ones with the caraway seeds are delicious, Diana. They're almond-flavored. Well, when his son took over the management, they lost everything. It was a disaster. Bankruptcy, you know. Harmon was never the same afterward.*" (212)

"Real life" (on tape), while Betsy comes at him with a knife, and in the old ladies' words is the mirror message: "*when the son took over the management, they lost everything. It was a disaster,*" just

8 Greenan will continue to zero in on America and violence in his later novels. In particular Betsy's sanguinary American acts seem to have left their influence on the "political" novels *La nuit du jugement dernier/Doomsnight* (some of whose characters were also once patrons of the Zero Inn where Ig meets Betsy) and *Dread of Night*.

as, contrary to expectations, Ig's taking charge (isn't this what boys need to do in order to become men?) and no longer tolerating his father's insane demands turn into a disaster.

> "Papa!" he yelled.
>
> The broad blade flashed in a short arc, struck the crown of his head with a morbid thump, and sent him writhing and twitching to the floor. His outstretched hands seized the blanket on the bed. The recorder tumbled down, silencing the two gossiping ladies. (212)

Ignacio Never—a murdered King, a sacrificed Christ, or just a fourteen-year-old boy caught in a coming-of-age tale, Greenan style.

CHAPTER THREE

"ALONE IN THE VOID": *THE SECRET LIFE OF ALGERNON PENDLETON* (1973)

> And the pigeons are still around.
>
> All imagination, perhaps. I'm alone too much.
>
> —*It Happened in Boston?* 140

And so is Algernon Pendleton, the narrator of Greenan's fourth novel, but you wouldn't believe it by his philosophy, which is a kind of reverse solipsism, in that everything outside the mind is alive with consciousness, and sometimes inhabited with the spirits of the dead. "Life and death," Al, the great-grandson of an eminent Egyptologist A. Edward Pendleton, writes at the beginning of his tale, an accounting of recent incidents, so "there will be no room for misinterpretation and no cause for them to think me a criminal" (25):

> Life and death. Is it possible that death, instead of being a state of nothingness, is nothing at all? I mean that it doesn't exist? That there is no death? Suppose everything is alive—this pen, this paper, my cigarette? A peculiar idea maybe, but one that I feel is worthy of serious consideration. My own belief is that we ourselves have been

> alive for many, many years—centuries, millennia or even more. We've occupied a variety of forms in a variety of situations on a multitude of other worlds. Only the frailty of memory prevents us from savoring these primeval experiences. Does the frog remember being a fish? Or the butterfly a caterpillar? No. It's a pity, really. (3–4)

Of course such beliefs allow him to justify murder, which leads him to commit another. Victims enter the Gothic labyrinth of his ancestral Brookline home, unaware of the Minotaur within.

Even so, Algernon is Greenan's most guilt-free protagonist, the most perversely charming of his mad narrators, and not because, as with other Greenan characters (Rev. Lenox, say, in *Heart of Gold*), he's a sociopath in-training or practice, but because of a specific event in his past, when the ship he was serving on during WWII was bombed and he was saved from drowning but not brain damage. As with Nabokov's *Lolita,* the reader of *The Secret Life of Algernon Pendleton* implicates himself whenever he identifies with the narrator/murderer (the authors give the reader little choice but to do so).[9]

Since both authors share a literary ancestor in Edgar Allan Poe, I need not insist here on conscious derivation. But it should be noted that, just as Vladimir Nabokov makes an anagrammatic appearance in *Lolita* as Vivian Darkbloom, Algernon is a near miss for his creator—lo, grenan—and Russell Greenan is split and twice quoted, once as Engenar—"*As sure as a parsnip is not a persimmon,/So is it certain, old men crave young women*"

9 Of course, even to call Humbert Humbert a murderer is to overlook, on the one hand, that his killing Quilty is a fantasy, a kind of auto-homicide, and on the other to diminish Humbert's larger crime, his treatment of Dolly.

(14) ("Engenar was sagacious," says Algernon, not yet knowing how wise the author of *Leonidas the King* is, since Algernon will be enamored of a young woman Madge Clerisy, an archaeologist after his great-grandfather's secrets)—and later as Sursell—"*Majestic change! Of all things the sum. / Without it, today is yesterday, / And bright tomorrow can never come.*"[10] These words are brought to mind when Algernon reflects outside the abandoned business of Mahir Suleyman, an antique dealer he has killed. "It's astounding how swiftly things can change, I thought to myself. In the space of a couple of months, a whole world—a small one, perhaps, but real and vital enough—had been obliterated. And how? By a single stroke of a walking stick! It was a sobering observation" (224).

The effect of sympathizing with Algernon—and we do, we do, brain-damaged as he is, hounded by creditors, conned by an academic, and badgered by Eulalia, the porcelain pitcher that talks to him—is like sympathizing with one of Poe's thoroughly unsympathetic murderers, the narrator of, say, "The Black Cat" who is possessed, you may recall, by the "spirit of PERVERSENESS":

> Of this spirit philosophy takes no account. Yet I am not more sure that my soul lives, than I am that perverseness is one of the primitive impulses of the human heart—one of the indivisible primary faculties, or sentiments, which give direction to the character of Man. Who has not, a hundred times, found himself committing a vile or a silly action, for no other reason than because he knows he

10 Poe also was a participant in the game of anagrams. Greenan's designs, as best as I can unscramble them, acknowledge the game but resists joining players like Nabokov on the word-golf links.

> should *not*? (*The Fall of the House of Usher and Other Writings* 322)

Poe's narrator cuts out the eye of his cat with his pen-knife and shortly thereafter hangs it from a tree. Later he will kill his wife ("I withdrew my arm from her grasp and buried the axe in her brain"), contemplate "cutting the corpse into minute fragments" (327), and eventually put the body in a wall in the cellar.

But it's not exactly the imp of the perverse that causes Algernon to murder his old Navy buddy Norbie Hess, the man who saved his life during the war when their ship is hit by a torpedo.[11]

> As vivid as reality the scene came back to me. A silver curtain of rain, lightning blinking in the distance, and suddenly the star shells burst. A mistake, I thought. Grabbing a poncho to throw over my head, I ran out onto the port wing of the bridge. The fragrance of flowers filled my nostrils—hibiscus, or night-smelling orchids, or maybe frangipani—wafted from the island by the storm's wind. Like an aurora the flares danced in the sky. I could perceive two APD's anchored offshore, and then, without the least translation of time, I found myself in the sea gagging on salt water, and my brain a brazen chime clanging in the belfry of my skull. (44)

Norbie saves him from drowning, but one after-effect of this event is that Al begins to hear voices. Persuaded by the logic of Eulalia, he will shoot Norbie Hess in the head and bury him in

11 Greenan's afterword to *IHiB?* notes that he "served in the Navy during the war" (2003, 278).

the Burying Ground behind his house in Brookline. He will also cane to death the Turkish antique dealer Mahir Suleyman and refuse to release Madge Clerisy from the secret room beneath the burial chamber of A. Edward Pendleton (A. E. P./ E. A. P./ E. A. Poe?). But before he commits these "understandable" deeds, he shoots, in a chapter entitled "The Waif," a blind puppy, again on the insistence of Eulalia, who is obviously (though not obvious to Algernon) jealous.

> Thus, on the day before Norbie came, I carried poor Homer down cellar and did what I had to do. While he rolled on his back with his paws dangling in the air and his stiletto-tipped tail wagging passionately, I fired my Navy .45 automatic into his head. There was no other course, really . . . Though the deed saddened me, I experienced no guilt. It was so marvelously swift; one second he was with me, and the next he was gone. I was also comforted by the incontrovertible belief that the little beast would attain elsewhere a sounder body than the one he was forsaking here. That was a silver lining to the cloud. (38–39)

A further silver lining is that Al can use the bones from the boiled dog for his osteo-art.

> Osteo-art, or the fashioning of sculpture from bones, is a cherished hobby of mine. Years back I read about it in a magazine, and having an abundant supply of ribs, vertebrae, shoulder blades and kneecaps ready to hand in the charnel house, I resolved to give it a whirl. I soon

turned out some creditable pieces, too. Once stimulated, it's astonishing how inventive even an untrained person can become. On my first attempt, using only a split thighbone and a scapula, I created a lovely sailboat. Afterward I made a tortoise from foot phalanges and a broken hipbone, and then a chess set—a strangely beautiful one—out of a batch of finger bones.

It's an absorbing pastime. (39)

—as is listening to this madman. The chess set of finger bones—an example of Greenan's comic macabre touch.

Other things talk to Al, among them pillows, philodendrons, dandelions, and a frog. The mad clerk who narrates Gogol's "Diary of a Madman" also suffers auditory hallucinations. "I'll confess that recently I have been seeing and hearing things that no one else has ever seen or heard" (Gogol 9).[12] The two talking, letter-writing dogs Madgie and Fidele in that story reveal information not only about the clerk's object of desire, Sophie the daughter of his Director, but also the clerk himself: "Sophie can hardly control her laughter when she sees him" (19). (A similar epistolary revelation occurs when Al finds out that his "lovely Madge" had described him as "a creepy individual—weak in the head from an old war wound . . . a prize booby" [206].) Eulalia goads Al to commit murder; natural objects, on the other hand,

12 Twice in his narration, Al refers to Gogol. If he bought a car, he thinks, "I could whirl about the countryside like Mr. Tchitchikov in his famous troika" (127). *Dead Souls,* concerned as it is with souls and saturated with death, is the right reference to find in *The Secret Life of Algernon Pendleton*. Later, after Madge has caught him talking to the pitcher, Al writes, "Only a Russian novelist—a Gogol or Dostoyevsky—could have described my humiliation" (155). Perhaps Al has in mind here the humiliation suffered by Akaky Akakievich in "The Overcoat" or Golyadkin in Dostoyevsky's Gogolian *The Double*.

are more likely to act as his conscience. Al has to take drives into the country because

> the house plants—the philodendrons—and the dandelions in the yard frequently insulted me. They insisted that I had killed Norbie for his money—an absolute calumny. Indoors or out, I was plagued by them. Only at night when they were sleeping could I be sure of tranquility. What liars they were! I seem to recall that Eulalia had shown an interest in the money at the time, but for me it had hardly existed. I have my faults, I admit, yet baseness isn't one of them. (180–81)

A few pages later, Al will murder one of these slandering philodendrons:

> I brought him back into the parlor and placed him on the butterfly table, got a pair of shears and set about clipping off his heart-shaped leaves. At once, his bravado left him. He yelped in pain and pleaded for mercy, but—and I'm ashamed to admit it—there was no compassion in me . . . And while I performed this savage little immolation, I grunted with satisfaction. (191–92)

In Part One, Chapter 16, Poe-like a jay outside his window calls "Wretch! Wretch! Wretch!" (71) which Al misreads as only insolence. And at the moment when he's busy using his philosophy to absolve himself from the murder he's about to commit ("The rite of absolution was superstition. Childishness. Both heaven and hell were misconceptions. Souls moved from world to world in the twinkling of an eye"), he again cannot read the "natural" signs. "The houseplants on the window sill began to whisper excitedly, though I wasn't able to distinguish what they said" (92).

Despite his belief that everything is alive always, that "Eternity is open to all" (246), Algernon Pendleton is, as the title of one of the novel's chapters has it, "alone in the void" of his madness. He has inklings of the truth of his condition and Madge Clerisy confronts him directly with it. "Instead of reading Einstein, Al," she tells him, "you should've looked into Freud. Your illness is one that he covers quite comprehensively. The china pitcher is only a prop—a kind of ventriloquist's dummy. It doesn't actually talk to you, but you talk to yourself through it. Do you understand?" But he refuses to accept this. And why should he? His belief that there exists "vast unexplored areas" that are beyond the limits of the most human senses is sufficient to him to explain his extrasensory powers and allows him to deny the isolation of his madness.

Late in his tale, he retreats to Hall's Pond behind his house and there sits with his shoes in the water like "two small rodents quenching their thirst" (211) and has what may be the book's strangest encounter. He hears a frog croak "Ragged! Ragged!" "Auditory hallucination—that's what you are! Go away, and take your ragged conversation with you," Al replies. When the "saucy devil" has the audacity to "physically appear" (211–12), Al asks him to tell him where he came from.

> "Egypt!" said the little fellow. "Egypt! Egypt!"
>
> "Egypt, you say? So that's it! Egypt, indeed!" I blew a stream of smoke in his direction, but it lost itself in the mist before reaching him. "You prove my point, frog. Egypt is inside my mind. Yes, it fills my thoughts—Egypt.

> And, therefore, you are an hallucination—do you see? You, poor soul, are only the echo and reflection of my . . . my . . . my weak-mindedness. Still, I'll be civil . . . and pretend. What brought you here, good sir?"
>
> "Hazard—ragged hazard," was his answer.
>
> "Ah! The circumstances were casual, and not causal, eh?" said I, leaning back on the bole of the tree, while extracting my well-moistened toes from the water.
>
> The amphibian surveyed me with heavy-lidded, tumescent eyes. "In Luxor . . . Luxor—on the margin of the Nile we lived," he said distinctly. (212)

After the frog tells Al his story about the coming of a one-eyed crocodile that devoured thousands of frogs, the croc itself appears and eats the story-teller. "Good God in heaven!" Al exclaims.

> "What does it mean? . . . What does it signify?"
>
> Out on the black surface the wisps of mist danced a macabre, measured ballet. (215)

The ebb and flow of Greenan's "macabre, measured ballet" in *The Secret Life of Algernon Pendleton* consists in part of Al finding himself in trouble, despairing, and then, by means of his philosophizing, finding contentment again, a pattern followed even in individual chapters, such as the "Alone in the Void" chapter which begins with Al sitting out in the Burying Grounds, after Madge has broken his precious porcelain Eulalia. "Of the numerous worlds in the universe . . . surely ours is the most terrible," he states (188). "Old, worthless, disgusting—that was how I felt. A pace away from where I sat there was a broken gravestone, its diagonal edge like that of a guillotine's blade. I considered smashing my skull on it" (189). But then Al's mind clears for a moment, as he "attempted to construct a philosophic barricade, hoping to regroup behind it the remnants of my routed dreams" (189). Al's philosophy is good enough to allow him to rationalize his killing the man who saved his life, but not good enough this time to overcome his despair at the death of Eulalia. Only a resurrection could (and does) do that.

How Al deals with his first murder and in turn kills Mahir Suleyman, an antiques dealer (assisted by "chance—that imp of the imponderable" [163]), and a philodendron, and leaves Madge Clerisy imprisoned in a secret chamber, in order to arrive at the book's end "[f]eeling elated" is this madman's achievement. "When I look back upon it now, the whole episode [of the first murder] seems an accident. I'm absolutely certain I never intended to shoot him—never! I was only playing with the notion—entertaining the philosophical possibilities of such an act" (92). A murder for altruistic reasons—Norbie is grossly overweight, sick, addicted to absinthe, in despair. No one ever dies. Sudden death is "desirable" (91).[13] These are the justifications Al gives for the following deed:

13 Before he shoots Norbie, Al recalls a work by De Quincey: "I found myself considering a story by Thomas De Quincey entitled 'The Vision of Sudden Death.' Although the substance of the tale evaded me, I did recall that it raised the interesting question of whether or not a quick end to life was desirable. The pagans felt it was, but the Christians—because of their concept of absolution—took the opposite view" (91–92). What Al is remembering are reflections by De Quincey in "Section II—The Vision of Sudden Death" of his half essay, half tale "The English Mail Coach":

> Caesar the Dictator, at his last dinner party [. . .], when the minutes of his earthly career were numbered, being asked what death, in *his* judgment, might be pronounced the most eligible, replied "That which should be most sudden." On the other hand, the divine Litany of our English Church, when breathing forth supplications, as if in some representative character, for the whole human race prostrate

> Well, a .45 is a cataclysmic firearm. In the little parlor it went off like a blockbuster, and the angle being what is was a portion of Norbie's bald crown flew up to the ceiling. Most of it ricocheted back down to the floor with a noise like crashing crockery, but an egg-shaped mass of gore remained up there, clinging to the calcimine. From it, drops fell. They appeared gray in color until they landed on my friend's sport shirt; there they bloomed into a radiant red.
>
> Despite my agitation, a line of Poe's forced its way into my consciousness. Somewhere he's written: "*And raining, it was rain; but having rained, it was blood.*" (93)

The simile "like crashing crockery" that foreshadows Madge's breaking of Eulalia; the delay of the information regarding whose "lump of brain" (26) Al sees fourteen chapters earlier; the comedy of the grotesque in a spot of "gore . . . clinging to the calcimine"—examples of Greenan's finesse in the art of fiction.

One also sees this finesse in the perfection of the novel's plot, how the chain of details lead exquisitely from one death to another until the final trap is sprung on the novel's femme fatale (Madge trapped in Al's great-grandfather's Egyptian-style tomb fifty feet beneath the charnel house where Al selects his bones for his osteo-art); in Greenan's terrible building which this time extends behind the house to the Charnel House and Burying

---

before God, places such a death in the very van of horrors: "From lightning and tempest; from plague, pestilence, and famine; from battle and murder, and from SUDDEN DEATH—*Good Lord, deliver us*." Sudden death is here made to crown the climax in a grand ascent of calamities; it is ranked among the last of curses; and yet by the noblest of Romans it was ranked as the first of blessings. (107–108)

Ground and Hall's Pond ("'A cemetery in your backyard,' Norbie remarks. 'That's weird! I suppose some of your relatives are buried in it.' 'A few,' Al replies." [73]); in the novel's carefully researched Egyptology; and in Al's language, his diction. Examples of the latter include (my italics) the "*incused* features" on Mahir Suleyman's coin-like face (10); Al's "*inditing*" instead of writing his story ("The reason I am inditing this story" [15]); Norbie's "*batrachian* visage" (59); Mahir "*pleached* his brown fingers in his lap" (79).

Often Al draws his analogies from his naval past, recalling for us each time the incident during the war that caused his madness: the Burying Ground with its "fifty-odd tombstones, tilted in every direction, resembled ranks of drunken sailors" (73); examining the corpse of Mahir, Al sees "from out of the darkness" of Mahir's partially open mouth that "the gold tooth winked at me, like a signal light blinking a nautical message across a nocturnal sea" (173). Greenan's observant eye, his avidity for detail, is on full display in this novel. Al's once-"pretty crown of hair" is now "a limp, yellow-gray mat—a morbid-looking object, like the pelt of a rodent" (16). "Norbie's bald crown was speckled with pearls of sweat" (67). After listening to Al's story of Roger Williams's grave, of how the roots of an apple tree devoured the corpse, Norbie explodes with laughter and "his huge eyes sparkled like globes of soda water" (76). And throughout there are the comic juxtapositions that keep us unbalanced and laughing over the abyss.

> Sometimes on clear nights when I survey the heavens, I am overcome with a violent—yes, violent—sensation of kinship for every one of my fellow creatures out in those limitless depths . . . Really, I am absorbed by it all. My soul

lunges across the light-years as easily as a hunter jumping a hedge. I am one with the whole of creation.

Before breakfast I spoke briefly with Eulalia. She displayed considerable interest in the sixty thousand dollars in Norbie's suitcase. (72)[14]

If the Greenan building consists of floors marked Insanity, Grimness, Horror, and Humor, it's the last level that's the most dangerous. Again in *The Secret Life of Algernon Pendleton* we have a Greenan character's death mistaken for a joke, in this case A. Edward Pendleton: "The morning we found him dead in his bed he still seemed so hale and hearty that we thought he was playing possum, since he was a notorious practical joker" (6). When Al says that without "Eulalia I might well have slipped off the rails, somewhere along the way" (25), we laugh, but what is the consequence of our laughter? "After living nearly a lifetime without digging a single grave, I was now about to scoop out my third in as many weeks" (173) is also a funny line. Recalling the gallows humor of old Burma Shave road signs, Al thinks: "Amusing, despite the grim themes. In those long-gone days people hadn't been so intense. Even death was a subject for comedy" (199).

The proof copy's title for this novel was "Cross Your Fingers, Hope to Die," a phrase Greenan plays with throughout the narrative by having Al cross his fingers whenever he needs to lie. But the title also suggests that we should hope (I'm crossing my fingers in the hope that . . .) we die. Better death than the hell of life in a Greenan novel.

Such a pleasant voice Algernon Pendleton has. When was the last time you encountered a Navy man who restricts his cursing

14 The first words we hear out of the pitcher's avaricious "mouth" are: "And did he pay as much as the last time?" (18).

to the rare "damn" or uses expressions like "Welladay"? How often Al sinks into despair, only to be brought out of it by his philosophy. The reader rides on the waves of his emotions, buoyed by the thought that his delusions will likely help him win out in the end. We genuinely like this brain-damaged murderer who feels more sympathy for a talking piece of porcelain than a woman trapped in his Great-grampy's tomb, even if she is a conniving, cold-blooded, career-driven academic. By the time we finish *The Secret Life of Algernon Pendleton*, Greenan has made sure the imp of the perverse resides as well in his readers.

CHAPTER FOUR

"A MYRIAD OF DISQUIETING CONSIDERATIONS": *HEART OF GOLD* (1975)

I. "An expression of rapturous greed"

In *The Secret Life of Algernon Pendleton* (1973), the narrator recalls these lines from Thomas Hood:

> *Gold! Gold! Gold! Gold!*
> *Bright and yellow, hard and cold.*
>
> *Gold, gold—alas! for the gold*
> *Spent where souls are bought and sold.*
>
> Think about it, Mahir had said. What else could I do but that? (150)

Many of Greenan's characters suffer the same obsession as Algernon Pendleton, among them the Reverend Dr. John Matthew Lenox in *Heart of Gold*, a Boston minister who leads a double life as Johnny Matthew, gambling and whoring when "off duty." One of his parishioners, an elderly Boston socialite named Geraldine Gargan, tells the story about Lenox's father, also a minister, giving last rites to the father of Amos Cavanaugh, the richest and most miserly member of Lenox's flock:

> "When the silver crucifix was pressed against his lips he opened his eyes and stared at it. Then, glancing up at your father, he mumbled something. 'What was that he said?' the physician asked. And with greatest reluctance, your poor father answered, 'Mr. Cavanaugh said, "Twelve dollars, sir. That's the best I can offer." '" (34)

Geraldine also says that, like his son Amos, Clarence Cavanaugh was an "odious creature. His whole character was permeated with greed. Toward the end of his life his face came to look like a mask of the devil. Really! He was the final evil distillation of the venom of usury" (33).

"Nicely put, my dear. Are these ladyfingers?" says Rev. Lenox esuriently, as usual alert first to his needs (ladyfingers, in this case) and the surface, not the substance, of the discussion.

In this stern black comedy, with its plot hinging on Amos Cavanaugh's wish to take his money with him into the afterlife, greed once again controls the game. Cavanaugh offers Lenox power-of-attorney over his estate in order to have his money transferred into bullion when he dies and then transported to the other side, a scheme that snares Cavanaugh when he reads an ad in the paper:

> CAN WEALTH BE TRANSFERRED
> TO THE HEREAFTER?
>
> Prof. Rupert Hofbauer, internationally famed physicist, will send interested parties a brief treatise on this vital

> subject. To cover cost, forward twenty-five cents to Prof. Hofbauer 194 Blagden St., Boston 02116. (6)

"It wouldn't be fair, wouldn't be justice," Cavanaugh tells Lenox, "to repossess a person's goods before the end of the world. That's how it seems to me." "Dotty as Cavanaugh was," Lenox thinks, "he had succeeded admirably in shoring up the flimsy structure of his avaricious dream" (8). When Cavanaugh elaborates on what he has learned about Hofbauer's method of transporting his wealth to the afterlife, all hocus-pocus sprinkled with antimatter, Lenox wonders "if the Otherside is heaven, where is hell?" The reader knows the correct answer, even if Lenox doesn't, at least not yet.

With a minister as the wicked protagonist, greed motivating the crime, devils in the air, ancestral evil and a house of Seven-Gables proportions ("The house was on Marlborough Street—a three-story brownstone whose intricately tailored cornices, consoles and pediments had all been ravaged by the abrasive onslaughts of a hundred Boston winters" [3]), *Heart of Gold* is Greenan's most Hawthorne-inflected novel. Melville saw "half of Hawthorne's soul . . . shrouded in a blackness, ten times black . . . This great power of blackness in him derives its force from its appeals to that Calvinistic sense of Innate Depravity and Original Sin, from whose visitations, in some shape or other, no deeply thinking mind is always and wholly free" (*The Piazza Tales* 243)—certainly not the mind of a sociopath like Reverend Lenox or one of his "innocent" parishioners, the family man, florist, and, alas, psychotic Jerry Gingerich.

Early in the novel, Gingerich (like the narrator of *It Happened in Boston?* and other Greenan characters, he has reveries of a sort) tries to explain to his pastor his need to do strange things. "Some of the ideas I get are so unusual," he tells Rev. Lenox. "I wonder if anybody in the world ever had them before . . . They say it's like a computer—the brain, I mean . . . Of course, as long as the brain is working all right, a person will never wander off that narrow, narrow road but with a tremendously complicated instrument, full of tiny components, an awful lot of things can go wrong—can't they, Reverend?" Lenox responds to his troubled parishioner that "the mind always has complete control. No matter who you are, you have to do what your brain commands. And the brain can command anything . . . anything it wants" (27).

To lure Cavanaugh out of his house to his death, Lenox, or rather the avaricious brain beneath his crown, lays a trail of dollar bills, as in a fairy tale, along the sidewalk and into the alley.

> At last Cavanaugh tottered into view . . . Tightly clutched in his hand, and looking like a bunch of fresh parsley, were the dollars that the minister had set out for him. An expression of rapturous greed was deeply imprinted on the old man's face, while his nose, like a quivering compass needle, pointed directly at the five-dollar bill on the ground before the doorway. When he stooped to pick it up, Lenox hit him on the head with the iron pipe . . .
>
> A crimson gout of blood flew from Cavanaugh's nostrils. His eyes, suddenly devoid of expression, bulged in their sockets. He took a step back, shuddered violently and fell sideways across the tilted lid of the garbage can. Thrice more, Lenox struck him. Under these ferocious blows the old man's head lost its symmetry, becoming as eccentric as a head reflected in the roiled surface of a fun-house mirror. Blood trickled down his temples to flood the

> creases in his leathery cheeks. He rolled slowly off the garbage can, landed on his face on the pavement, wriggled convulsively onto his back, straightened both legs as if to make himself more comfortable, and then was perfectly still. In each of his hands he held money: in his left, the cluster of one-dollar bills, and in his right, the single crumpled five. With the blood now running into his gaping mouth, he gazed blankly up at the clouded sky. (74)

Cavanaugh's death, another in a line of Grand Guignol Greenan set pieces, is emblematic of the fate of the avaricious in this novel. Lenox will also bludgeon to death a pair of con artists, and, a con artist himself, have his throat slit. Is this the fate all confidence men deserve? Well, not everyone who plays the confidence game is enraptured by glitter.

II. "*The Prince of Condom*"

Enter Mary Urquhart, a fortyish Boston bag lady of the first order. She prattles, she puns, she drinks like a fish. She's an erudite, sociable con artist, the sort who bums for the art of the game, not the score. From Lenox she'll extract only a few bills, with no intention of paying them back, though in the end she will, and with an exorbitant return on his investment. "Her face, though pleasant, bore signs of a sensual and intemperate disposition." To Reverend Lenox she says she has "the hope and modest expectation that you'll be able to provide me with a little spiritual comfort and temporal succor" (56). Lenox, troubled but not fully appreciating "the peculiar emphasis his caller had put on the word 'succor,'" lets her in.

What troubles him about that word? That he knows the succor he offers his parishioners is a sham and Mary's spin on the word acknowledges this? Or that he picks up the implied *sucker* and worries she's about to make him one? "Why the crafty old boozer!" Lenox says when, his twenty dollars tucked into her pocket, he sees her walk off, "[a]ll evidence of her limp . . . vanished," only to be caught by "the reflection of his startled features in the glass pane," at which "he laughed softly and turned away" (60)—missing the message in the reflection that it's he who is the con man, though not in the end any more successful than Hofbauer, and he who soon enough will sink into the bottle, a victim of that "instrumentality of the Fiend Intemperance," as Poe has it in "The Black Cat" (*The Fall of the House of Usher* 321).

Mary may at first seem like only another exhibit in Greenan's gallery of eccentrics, as well as a scam artist in a book already filled with them. Few characters in *Heart of Gold* aren't either a con or a victim of the same, especially among the principals. Reverend Lenox fleeces his parishioners, steals from his church's accounts, and seduces Lucia, the niece of the "old miser" Amos Cavanaugh, who has made his fortune, like his father before him, as an unscrupulous usurer and falls victim in turn to Professor Hofbauer's scam. As much as in *It Happened in Boston?* or *Huckleberry Finn* or West's *The Day of the Locust*, the universe of *Heart of Gold* is permeated with cheaters. Even Lenox, unable to detect the subterfuge behind Hofbauer's "weird little Charge Translator" that can send objects to the "Otherside," for a moment believes "it must all be true. It had to be. The professor was genuine."

> "What a terrifying notion!" the minister mumbled. "It means that anything is possible . . . anything at all."

> He shot a quick look at the milky-blue sky over Beacon Hill, as though hoping to fathom with the naked eye the billions of light-years of space that lay in that direction.
>
> "There might even be a God," he said tremulously. (176)

The unbeliever posing as a believer is conned, albeit briefly, into belief.

"The Prince of Condom," Mary calls her first lover, a "conscienceless con man" with a mouth "full of deceit and falsehoods" (139). Trained, then, in her craft by a professional, Mary is a master scammer with a talent for composing letters of request for financial aid and with a wit as scatological as Rabelais's. "That's a Scottish name—Urquhart. Sounds like a rude noise, doesn't it?" (58). But it's also a name with a heart in it, and her forename is replete with religious ancestry. "The woman really should be on the stage," Lenox says, but Mary, it will turn out, has a role to play beyond that of simply another Greenan vaudevillian.

III. *"The human brain is a funny instrument"*

After Cheeks, one of Lenox's gambling buddies, tells him that Hofbauer is really a grifter named Gus Vogel, Lenox realizes that the Otherside, God, and the Devil are "simply hokum" (201). But the universe of *Heart of Gold* is so deceptive and full of deception, even this revelation can't go unquestioned. So deceived, epistemologically limited, and ethically compromised are Greenan's characters, the reader finds it difficult to trust his own conclusions.

In a world of liars lying to liars, cons conning cons ("Hofbauer was too confirmed a liar to have any faith in the veracity of others"

[205]), what place is there for morality? “Even your goddamn gun is phony!” Lenox shouts, holding Vogel’s plastic pistol, before he proceeds to bludgeon Vogel to death. The same fate, immediately thereafter, awaits Vogel’s female accomplice, at the end of which Lenox is “drenched in gore” (211).

What impresses Lenox about his murders is how logical and clear-headed he remains throughout them. “Throughout his exertions, the minister’s brain had functioned remarkably well. From the instant Hofbauer had pulled the fake gun he seemed to know, almost by instinct, exactly what he should do. Even when the blonde woman had entered the house, even when he was frenziedly beating her, there hadn’t been any uncertainty or confusion in the busy corridors of his mind” (212).

“The human brain is a funny instrument,” says the florist and family man Jerry Gingerich to Lenox as they stand on the sidewalk in front of an aquarium, whose glass pane, Lenox notes, Gingerich is using to watch him, not the fish.

> “It’s full of circuits and gadgets, and the nervous system shoots out of it like wires . . . I’ve had times when my brain seems to stop working . . . It becomes empty . . . The brain becomes a void . . . You feel dead . . . completely dead . . . as if your soul is dead, too. Obliterated. And the worse part is that you’re somehow conscious of what’s happened . . . I wish I could describe what it’s like. I can’t though. Words are . . . just words. They’re ideas, words—not feelings. You can have the word ‘fear’ in your mind, but that doesn’t mean you’re afraid, does it? Terror, panic—they don’t come close to the reality. True terror is huge. It’s a gigantic world—one that very few people know

> about. Most human beings are like those fish. They believe the world is the size of an aquarium. They don't know what's outside their own little fishbowl . . . but I know. Maybe it's just as well that I can't give a good description, Reverend, because if I could—if I could paint a clear picture of nonexistence for you—well, for the rest of your life you might keep thinking about it. You might not think of anything else." (182–83)

We've been at this promontory where Gingerich stands many times before in literature, in Büchner's *Woyzeck*, for example, in Poe's "The Imp of the Perverse": "We stand on the brink of a precipice. We peer into the abyss—we grow sick and dizzy" (*Complete Tales and Poems* 282). It's the attraction of the vortex, the mirror to some, Melville's "dumb blankness, full of meaning" (*Moby-Dick* 212). Soon enough Gingerich will fall in; others, like Lenox, have already fallen but don't know it. Unable to convince Gingerich that he should go back to his psychiatrist Dr. Lifkin, Lenox heads off to a social engagement, where he finds it difficult "to be sociable . . . as his mind was preoccupied with a myriad of disquieting considerations" (185).

The mind is a funny instrument, all right, rich and varied and lost in a fishbowl all its own. Gingerich makes a final appeal to his minister for help before he slaughters his family. He tells Lenox over the phone that the brain is "a hub in a wheel. The rim of the wheel's the body, and the hub and the rim are connected by these little strings—like spokes . . . All your feelings and dreams travel along those strings, the way electricity flows through wires" (214). And now the "string cutters" are cutting all his wires.

According to Lenox, Lucia's "mind was a jumble of crazed fantasies, half-baked notions about good and evil" (249). She suffers from a different disorder—visions of Christ and demons—and believes a demon killed her uncle, though she doesn't know yet the demon is the man with whom she's fallen in love and had sex. Not that she's worried about the demons. "Morning, noon and night, I can feel God near me," she tells Lenox, "and while He's by my side, how can any of them touch me?" (194). A touching naïveté, one might say, if it weren't for the fact that Lucia, seduced and duped by Lenox, will hang herself from a tree in her uncle's backyard when she realizes that the demon after all has touched her—touched even her heart.

One of Lucia's religious experiences curiously connects to Jerry Gingerich's last take on the mind as the hub of a wheel. She tells Lenox that "the most important" of these events

> "happened outside a doughnut shop in Lynn. That changed me completely. What happened was I opened the trunk of my car to get a pack of cigarettes, and inside the spare tire I saw the head of Jesus."
>
> "In the spare tire?"
>
> "Exactly. It was in the middle . . . hanging there . . . floating. The tire was like a picture frame for it." (157)

Later, Lenox's own crossed wires will cause him to imagine that "she could be planning to sell him for silver, like a damn Judas Iscariot" (250), which odd turn would make Reverend Dr. John Matthew Lenox Jesus Christ.

A plea for a certain kind of irrationality seems to be at work in *Heart of Gold*. For Melville, "it is not the brain that can test such a man [as Hawthorne]; it is only the heart. You cannot come to know greatness by inspecting it; there is no glimpse to be caught of it, except by intuition; you need not ring it, you but touch it, and you find it is gold" (*The Piazza Tales* 244). The only time Lenox's quite different heart of gold is touched is when such rationality breaks down. "In that instant a strange irrational notion took possession of Lenox's mind. He wanted to throw the pipe away and clasp the injured man in his arms. It was like a mad revelation . . . He wanted to comfort him, to assure the frightened old fellow it was all a terrible mistake" (73). But Lenox's rationality wards off revelation, even though examples of rationality's limits are there for him to learn from. The detective who believes Gingerich killed Cavanaugh, Lenox sees has reason on his side. "This sleuth's reasoning was perfectly sound, all right, but the result was nonsense. How odd it should work out so neatly" (231).

IV. "*. . . and why must he keep thinking of hell?*"

How rational, how sane Reverend Lenox looks beside Gingerich or Lucia, or even Cavanaugh, Hofbauer/Vogel, and Mary Urquhart. No visions of Jesus in a hubcap has Lenox, no demons or "string cutters" haunt him, and surely he's a better con man than Cavanaugh or Vogel. At rationalizing away murder, he's as adept as Algernon Pendleton. While reworking (i.e. plagiarizing, stealing) one of his father's sermons:

> The notion of murder, like a bit of jetsam from one of his cruising daydreams, kept bobbing around in the dark sea of his consciousness.
>
> Murder. There were reasons to ponder it. Cavanaugh never should have said, "Maybe I'll . . . live another dozen

> years." That was imprudent—almost insolent. He, Lenox, would be middle-aged in another dozen years.
>
> Murder. Surely the rewards outweighed the risks. As to morality—the scoundrel was seventy-nine. He had no right to twelve more years. Did he want to live forever?. . . What's more, he was ill—close to death. A single nudge and the affair could be neatly resolved.
>
> Nor was murder, despite popular belief, one of those exacting enterprises that an inexperienced man might be wary of attempting. Inept and ignorant folk performed the sly deed every hour on the hour, and damn seldom were they caught. Why, the daily newspapers were sodden with gore: cadavers in rivers, automobiles, alleys, in tenements and penthouses, in lover's lanes, in gunnysacks and steamer trunks. It was a thriving recreation.
>
> Murder—yes. He had the nerve to accomplish it, too, though it would have to be arranged in a coldly impersonal way. Amos need not see his assassin . . . Lenox felt squeamish about this. To face his victim, to reveal his identity under those circumstances, would be an excessive hardship for both of them, he was convinced. He must strike him down from behind. Let the old devil imagine that he died at the hands of Nemesis. (55–56)

"To face his victim . . . would be an excessive hardship for both of them"—does our minister possess a modicum of conscience, a soupçon of scruples? At the funeral for Gingerich's wife and two sons—having received no succor from Lenox, Gingerich killed them—Lenox, who performs the service, "was more upset by the destruction of the small family than by the murders he himself had committed with his own hands" (226). Also, Lenox is relieved when a New York drifter is cleared of murdering Vogel and his accomplice.

What an interesting sociopath our minister is. Unlike Cavanaugh, who is driven by a genetic sin of greed, Lenox's crimes have no such Hawthornean base. To Lucia he complains about how hard Christmas was for him and his mother because his father gave everything to the church (a mistake his son will not repeat), but this hardly seems equal to a Salem judge's crimes or Original Sin. Nonetheless, Lenox is willing to allocate guilt to the father for the crimes of the son. "Hadn't he insisted that his son be a minister? Yes—and by so doing, he had planted the seed of the murder many years ago. Why now should he complain of the bitter fruit? The sins of sons, say what you will, are all derived from foolish fathers" (97).

The mind, the mind, what a funny instrument it is, what a labyrinth of reason, edifice of nonsense, built to withstand morality, but easily penetrated by demons and devils.

> *O hoofed and hornéd Lord,*
> *Thou sly and subtle liar;*
> *O scaly fright,*
> *O Prince of Night,*
> *Behind thy fence of fire.*
>
> Where had he ever learned that? he wondered—and why must he keep thinking of hell? (127)[15]

In a world where greed and charlatans (demons, devils) reign, it's not hard to see Hofbauer/Vogel's anti-world as the real world and

15 Perhaps an original poem by one of Greenan's near anagrams.

"our" world as a Gnostic one akin to Alfred Omega's vision in *It Happened in Boston?* where the only solution to ultimate despair of reality is to dethrone God. But Vogel and his Charge Translator's link to the Otherside are only a con.

In the end it's Mary Urquhart's act of Christian charity, so to speak, that will send Lenox to his demise. She is, after all, with her conning letters that serve as a sort of a promotional campaign for giving and with her own giving (social, sexual) self, the novel's most Christian character. She's never spent the spoils of her scams, and when Lenox finds a bag in her apartment filled with money, Mary gladly offers it to him. "Do you need money, lamb? . . . Are you paying attention to me, you handsome devil? Do as Mary says. Take the whole thing—you hear? Use it for good works" (273). What luck. Lenox, now in possession of all the money he needs to leave the country, returns to his church, only to meet his doom in Gingerich, who slits Lenox's lamb-like throat.

> "Wait!" the minister begged. "Jerry . . . wait . . . wait. Please. Only another minute!"
>
> But even as he cried out, his head was yanked back by the hair and the knife entered his throat. He felt the blade tearing through his flesh, tasted the hot blood in his mouth, felt his mind dissolving in the awful, fiery pain.
>
> Then it ended. It was all over—and in this world, Lenox suffered no more. (276)

The suggestion is there, but Greenan refrains from italicizing the *this* in "this world." But whose hand is at work, the author's or a retributive God's, or the author's as a stand-in for the same, that allows Mary to combine in her patter two of the novel's key motifs—the clock and fire? The former is what Lenox mistakes as the face of the clock he sees in Cavanaugh's window after he has killed the miser, when in fact it's the face of Vogel's female accomplice. The latter—well, Lenox does say "I don't mind heat" (151). "A man doesn't pay much attention to the clock on the mantel when he's busy poking the fire," Mary says. "Ha, ha! It's true, Reverend, absolutely true. I wouldn't feed a line to a Christian" (269). And it's unlikely she has.

On the way back from the funeral of the Gingerich family, Lenox, crying, thinks, "What a raw deal life is! How cruel and idiotic! . . . "*O that I had wings like a dove—for then I would flee away, and be at rest.* Life is a senseless misery" (227). What the good reverend is quoting from is Psalms 55:6, but Greenan also expects us to know the two verses which precede it:

> My heart is sore pained within me: and the terrors of death are fallen upon me.
>
> Fearfulness and trembling are come upon me, and horror hath overwhelmed me.
>
> And I said, Oh that I had wings like a dove! *for then* would I fly away, and be at rest.

And he may also want us to recall Psalms 68:12 ("Though ye have lien among the pots, *yet shall ye be as* the wings of a dove covered with silver, and her feathers with yellow gold"), just as Henry James, referencing this verse in his title, wants us to remember Psalms 55:4–6.

My mentioning James, who also knew well the power of gold, is not to say that *Heart of Gold* owes to James what it does to Hawthorne, but it is to acknowledge the continuum in American literature to which Greenan belongs.

CHAPTER FIVE

THE DEVIL TO PAY IN THE PARADIGM: *THE BRIC-A-BRAC MAN* (1976)

I. *In the Paradigm*

The Bric-a-Brac Man, in that it draws extensively from Greenan's experiences as an antique dealer in Boston in the 1950s and '60s, is perhaps the most autobiographical book by this non-autobiographical author.[16] In his afterword to the 2003 reprint of *It Happened in Boston?* he notes the importance of his bric-a-brac background to his first novel.

---

16 Asked why his childhood memories of growing up in the Bronx don't show up in his fiction, specifically in *It Happened in Boston?* Greenan told his interviewer, "The boy from the Bronx is in the book, but unless you knew that boy well it might take some hunting to find him" ("A Conversation with Russell H. Greenan"). And in his afterword to *Boston?* he states clearly his aesthetic regarding autobiographical fiction:

> What authors put down on paper springs from their own personal experiences, from all the memories that have gathered over the years in the recesses of their minds, not to mention all the books they have read. Naipaul says that if you want to know who a writer is you don't read his autobiography, you read his fiction. Autobiographies are full of lies, but storytelling strips you bare. A wise author will never explain his novel. He will tell you the novel explains him. (276)

> For a few years I was a traveling salesman in Maine, New Hampshire, and Vermont, but, ever restless, I quit the machinery company and opened an antique shop in Harvard Square, hoping to set up a business that someone else could eventually run for me. On the imagined profits from this operation I could then go to Europe and write a novel. The imagined profits remained that way, however, and my Cambridge venture failed. I opened another store called Back Bay Bric-a-Brac on Newbury Street, Boston's art-gallery district. Much of the material and atmosphere in *It Happened in Boston?* derives from those days, from the time I spent dealing with pickers, auctioneers, artists, restorers, and other members of the antique fraternity. But Back Bay Bric-a-Brac, despite its catchy name, did not succeed, either, and by then I was thirty-three, in debt, and married with three children. (278–79)

Arnold Hopkins, the eponymous figure and narrator of Greenan's sixth novel, dreams of "establish[ing] a magnificent gallery on New York's Fifth Avenue just down from the Plaza. Such was my recurring fantasy. Rengane [another Greenan anagram] wasn't wrong when he said:

> *Insatiable vanity?*
> *It's worse than stark insanity.*" (10)

Greenan and Hopkins may share a profession but little else. Hopkins, for example, is divorced and has no children. All that's left of his family is a first cousin, Maurice Fitzjames, his almost exact double. "Yes, except for a difference in the shade of our brown eyes, and a minor variation in the shape of our jaws, we were duplicates—genuine Doppelgängers" (5). Maurice, however, is a successful dealer, and the two cousins' relationship has consisted of one attempting to out-con the other. So far, Arnold Hopkins is the loser.

Almost everyone in *The Bric-a-Brac Man* in some way is part of the antique trade.[17] Even old ladies masquerading as customers turn out to be crooks. Arnold thinks he's sold the landlord of his newly opened antique shop $3,200 worth of merchandise only to find out that the landlord has conned him into letting movers take away the goods without giving Hopkins a check. "The whole deal had a strongly mephitic aroma" (108), thinks Arnold, not aware how apt the comparison is. Reflecting on the members of his profession, Hopkins writes, "We were modern men, which is to say, malcontents, cynics, misanthropes, Machiavels and renegades" (32). A milieu, then, that breeds avarice, masquerade, and crime, not unlike that of, say, the thieves' world as depicted by Fielding in his *The Life of Mr. Jonathan Wild the Great* (1743), based loosely on the eighteenth-century murderer and thief Jonathan Wild. Sentiments such as the following expressed by Hopkins one might easily find in Fielding's novel: "Life, however, is nothing if not perfidious and pernicious. If you indulge yourself in truth-telling—even a minute measure of it—sooner or later you'll be made to suffer for your folly" (58).

Moments occur, however, in *The Bric-a-Brac Man* when the trading in old goods seems to have some charm beyond avarice,

17 Bostonian Humphrey Flanagan, the main character of Greenan's tenth novel *Magique micmac/Glamour Doom* (2002) (another dark comedy: in one scene a character is hacked to death with a Boy Scout ax wielded by a bag lady named Tinker Bell), is also an antique dealer.

though these moments don't last for long. "Antique dealers," Hopkins tells us while listening to Maurice tell him about a house filled with artifacts he wants Arnold to steal,

> are a passionate breed—like gamblers, misers, libertines and poets. The mere description of a table or chair is often enough to set their hearts aflame. And it's not just a matter of money, either. Such emotions transcend price and profit. They're probably sublimated forms of lust. The dealer's hunger to possess exceptional merchandise, even though he may be aware that he can possess it for only a short while, is no less ferocious than the lover's drive to possess the beloved. So, as my cousin prattled on, I grew increasingly itchy with desire. (60)

For the most part we see the dealers busy trying to make a good score, by lying, stealing, or sharing trade secrets with one another on how to restore furniture, con customers and others, the post office, for example, by collecting insurance on pre-damaged goods. "I once read that the Greek god of commerce, Hermes, was also the god of cunning, eloquence, fraud, perjury and theft. Very astute, those Greeks," Hopkins says (87).

To varying degrees all of Greenan's previous novels spin out from a combination of Fate, often in the form of an encounter, and financial stress. Usually it doesn't take long for the protagonist to move into criminal activity to alleviate his stress, though it takes longer for the fateful encounter to play its plot cards. Inevitably what begins as a problem turns into a farce of bad luck, and the farce shifts into nightmare, and the nightmare darkens—theologically, metaphysically—into fantasy or madness or death. Alfred Omega of *It Happened in Boston?*, Stephen Pierglass of *Nightmare*,

Ignacio Never of *The Queen of America*, Algernon Pendleton of *The Secret Life of Algernon Pendleton*, Reverend Lenox of *Heart of Gold*—only the patterns within the paradigm vary.[18]

Having picked up for $700 a number of Japanese figurines from one of the tenants in 643 Commonwealth Avenue, a building where he does the odd repair for the eccentrics housed there, Arnold Hopkins unloads them on a dealer for $7000, with the promise the dealer will pay him the next day. Alas, he forgets to write up an invoice for the merchandise and the dealer dies (heart attack/car crash) after leaving Arnold. Also, his bank account, conveniently located in an out-of-state bank, has insufficient funds to cover the original $700. That's the problem, one further complicated by Hopkins's suffering from blackouts. "What triggers these spells evidently is overwork and worry, of which I have more than my share" (9).

And the fateful encounter? Three young women step out of the building at 645 Commonwealth Avenue. "Sisters, I said to myself—the three fates, turning up on cue to resurrect my failing fortunes" (11). A "wayward breeze" lifts "the veil of one of the women" and Hopkins is stunned. "I sat on the bench, scarcely breathing. The face beneath the veil had been incredibly beautiful. Inside my chest, my heart was pounding frantically" (11–12). It will take some time before this encounter plays its final cards in the novel's narrative game. Meanwhile Hopkins has to deal with the more pressing issue of money, and where there's money, morality can't be long for this world.

---

18 "The novels are plot-driven stories where a central character is drawn inexorably into a predicament that exposes the brittleness of human equanimity and the delusion of self-determination. The structure of a Greenan story hinges, as in ancient Greek tragedy, on a reversal of fortune as likely to be caused by a fatal mistake or *hamartia* as by a flaw of character." (http://en.wikipedia.org/wiki/Russell_H._Greenan)—an accurate description of the Greenan paradigm.

When Barney Slocum, another dealer, offers Hopkins a thousand dollars to burgle an apartment for a jeweled crucifix ("a seventeenth-century Italian ormolu job encrusted with lapis, carnelians and jargoons"), Hopkins doesn't waste time on the ethics of the matter. "I drank two mouthfuls of bourbon, reflecting cynically that crime was really only business carried on by other means. Then I put down my glass and said, 'Okay, I'll try it'" (42). Breaking into other people's homes offers Hopkins the illusion of autonomy. "I found, oddly enough, that this furtive work was rather pleasant. Violating the sanctity of a private home gave me a bizarre sense of power. Stepping boldly into a stranger's personal territory made me feel that I had at last achieved some control over my own destiny—that I was a manipulator instead of a manipulatee. It was exhilarating" (44).

As long, that is, as it's successful, and hasn't yet slipped into farce. Caught trying to escape from an apartment, Arnold clings to a plank he'd set up from one building to the next.

> I looked down, and the instant I did I became giddy. The sight of all that totally empty space—no awnings, clotheslines, trees or anything else—caused my brain to rotate slowly in my skull. At the bottom of this absolutely incredible abyss, the courtyard was a tiny oblong, pallid in the wan moonlight. I was aghast. I could barely breathe. It was like being on the end of a diving board, a hundred feet above a drained swimming pool—with someone tugging on your ankle.
>
> "Let go, you fool!" I croaked in terror. (51)

With the husband shaking the plank and the wife throwing cosmetic jars at him, Arnold is the comic fool dangling over the abyss:

"Beset by a multiplicity of evils, I didn't know what to do" (51). Then one of the jars hits him, and he shouts back at the couple: "'You're lunatics!' I bellowed. 'You're both crazy—homicidal maniacs. You want to kill me for aknickknack!'" (52).

After his escape, the farce continues when he answers the phone of a fellow dealer Hogan Guilfoyle, and posing as Guilfoyle, arranges to meet Lydia Crabtree and Elvira Lambert, two sisters who wish to sell him furniture. These two ladies ("It seemed to me that lately I was encountering more than my share of cuckoo birds" [82]), tell Hopkins that Lydia's son Tyrone has been accused of defenestrating his father, Lydia's late husband, because his father said he was going to buy a cat. "The poor boy can't bear to have cats anywhere near him, and his father knew that perfectly well, so why would he buy a cat? Ridiculous . . . Believe it or not, just a pussy willow is enough to bother him—and caterpillars give him hysterics" (83). Looking at a photograph of Tyrone, Arnold observes:

> Often, in the past, I had heard people described as having a "bullethead," but until that moment I'd never come across an authentic example of this phenomenon. Tyrone's broad skull really did look like something you could fire from a cannon. It was cylindrical and sloped upward to a point, though the torpedo effect was spoiled a bit by his fringe of wavy hair. As for his face, that was unprepossessing in the extreme. The eyes were small and piggish, and the nose was as crooked as a dog's hind leg. A tight smile curved his mouth, but the rest of his features wore an expression of smoldering menace. (83)

Conned by these two old ladies into waiting a few hours before he picks up the furniture, Arnold sees from a café across the street the furniture he's already paid cash for being put into a U-Haul by Tyrone. Everyone ahead of him at the cashier is paying with ten-dollar bills, so all he can do is watch the furniture be driven away. "Incredible! I thought. Who can you trust? Even old ladies are turning to crime" (87). On this farcical encounter a nightmare turns when Tyrone defenestrates the real Hogan Guilfoyle. It leads also in the end to the death of Maurice Fitzjames and—hey presto!—a reversal in the fortunes of our narrator. Or so it seems, for another fateful encounter, one worthy of and similar to the meeting at the opening of Bulgakov's *The Master and Margarita*, puts this ending in doubt.

II. *The Devil to Pay*

> "You want to borrow five hundred dollars?" [Guilfoyle] said. "Get it from the Devil."
>
> Then he laughed softly, as though the remark were a sparkling witticism.
>
> I muttered an oath and walked out. (35)

Offhand, casual, a joke. But in a Greenan novel jokes can come back to bite you. And so can the Devil, whom we possibly met in *It Happened in Boston?* as Mr. Beels (Beelzebub), an insurance salesman who tells the narrator that death "is the super-salesman of the insurance business" (99) and whose assistant is Johann, as in Johann Faust. In *The Bric-a-Brac Man* the Devil we meet may or may not be the real Devil, Hopkins is unsure whether he is a mad Mexican or the real thing. Thirty-four pages after Guilfoyle suggests Arnold get money from the Devil, he mentions him (or Him) again. "You could get the money from the Devil; he wouldn't expect it back" (69). According to Guilfoyle, there's

> "this crazy spic who thinks he's the Devil. Told me that if I signed a contract with this nutcase, he'd pay me real money."
>
> "What sort of contract?"
>
> "A contract for your soul. The Devil is always in the market for souls. Don't you know nothing about religion? . . ."
>
> "But suppose he actually is the Devil, Hogan? What then?"
>
> "Ha, ha, ha!" Guilfoyle laughed hoarsely. "That's an idea, ain't it? Maybe I should've checked with the archbishop before sticking my name on the contract. Only, if that ding-a-ling is the Devil, I must be the Virgin Mary." (69–70)

That Guilfoyle, the one true Catholic in the book, tells Hopkins on the day Guilfoyle dies that he has dreamed of his death, and that Hopkins is responsible for Tyrone Crabtree mistaking him for Hopkins—both of these events give Hopkins pause, especially since he, like Guilfoyle, has sold his soul to the Devil. "Is the Devil really the Devil? I wonder. Hogan Guilfoyle signed a contract with him, and not long after, he died. Then I signed one, and what happened? I was shot at, almost thrown off a roof, and narrowly missed being burned alive" (210).

But before all that happens Arnold needs money, and so pays a visit to Felix Jerónimo Rodríguez Diego de Merendaro y Alcalá, who introduces himself as the Devil, speaks in British locutions and collects British tea towels with the likenesses of, among others, King Edward the Eighth and Guy Fawkes. "The Guy Fawkes is even more valuable than the Edward the Eighth," says Merendaro. "Indeed, there is only one other pictorial tea towel that is of superior worth in the entire world, and that is a Jonathan Wild. I, alas, have never even seen a Jonathan Wild, because there exists only three of them. It illustrates him hanging on the scaffold at Tyburn" (73). After hearing out Arnold's request for money, the Devil says, "You wish to sell your soul, Mr. Hopkins. Jolly good. The question is, how do you feel about original sin? Do you believe people can be guilty even when they are innocent babies, and before they perpetrate any transgression?" No, Arnold says, "original sin is a postulate I can't accept." "Interesting. And free will? What are your opinions precisely with regard to that philosophical question? Would you endorse that people control all the events and episodes of their own little lives?" (74).

> "Free will is a myth, a fantasy, a mirage, a figment of the imagination. The true principle is willy-nilly. Each gesture we make, thought we think, sensation we feel is preordained. Human beings are simply automatons, robots programmed ages ago by a concatenation of dispassionate cosmic accidents." . . .
>
> The Devil lowered his small body onto a shaggy vermilion scatterrug on the floor, and reverting to his normal dulcet tone, said, "'A concatenation of dispassionate cosmic accidents.' Sublime, Mr. Hopkins. I immensely enjoy such orotundity. You have a way with a phrase, you really do. Instead of a purveyor of antiques, you should be a politician . . . Yet do you not recognize that the word 'cosmos' means order? Yes, yes—it means regularity or

> harmony. Thus a cosmic accident would be an ordered disorder, you see. How, sir, do you explain and reconcile this paradox?"
>
> "Ah, but the accidents I had in mind were those that produced the cosmos in the first place—the primary causes of the universe itself," I answered grandly . . .
>
> "Sir, I do not wholly understand," said Satan . . . "If, as you appear to suggest, accidents account for the universe, what function is there for God?"
>
> "None," I said promptly. "In my view there is no God. God is as much a fantasy as free will." (74–75)

The Devil refuses Hopkins's request "[b]ecause you are a nonbeliever, and in hell I have a vast superfluity of nonbelievers . . . How can you be faithless if you profess no faith? How can you be an outlaw if you are convinced that the universe is devoid of laws?" (75–76). Caught by the Devil's logic, Arnold is disappointed. "'There's something wrong with the world,' I said peevishly, 'when a man can't sell his soul to the Devil'" (76). Still, a soul is a soul, and they settle for $2000 to purchase Arnold's. The contract is a mixture of languages, many "impossible to identify," but "[a]ny qualms I might have felt were swiftly dissipated by the sight of the money in his small hand" (77).[19]

19 The Devil in *The Bric-a-Brac Man* and the insurance salesman Beels (Beelzebub) in *It Happened in Boston?* are, if not the same character, at least close cousins. Both devil figures, for example, possess polyglot accents. Felix Merendaro's "pronunciation was peculiar. He stressed the wrong words in his sentences and accented the wrong syllables, and his vowel sounds were all slightly askew" (72). Also, the contract Hopkins signs begins in English, but "lapsed after the opening lines into a polyglot jumble. There were words in German, Spanish, Arabic, Greek, French, Hebrew, and many other languages impossible to identify" (77). Mr. Beels's speech, the narrator of *It Happened in Boston?* tells us, "was marred by an accent, though I was at a loss to identify

What passes as Greenan's comic and realistic take on the antique trade ("my throat ached from conning and bargaining" [10]) darkens ("Money and murder aren't exactly strangers to each other in this world," Hopkins tells Barney Slocum [198]), and the Christian references begin to shape the novel more and more into a dark Greenan allegory. "Where should I start?" the novel begins. "A tricky question, that. God alone knows where all personal dramas begin, and though He's supposed to be omnipresent, He never seems to be around when you need Him" (3). God may or may not be absent in the universe of *The Bric-a-Brac Man*, but signs left over from the Judeo-Christian world are everywhere. After settling with an old woman to purchase her carved ivory pieces for a very low fee, Hopkins, while "[s]itting down to write the check, . . . caught sight of my face in a mirror, and Jesus on the cross had a happier expression. A few minutes later I carried the two cartons of ivories out to the station wagon. Only then did I grin" (16). When Hopkins moves into the basement apartment of 643 Commonwealth Avenue to be closer to 645 Commonwealth Avenue, the home of the three Ramsay sisters (the three Fates he's seen earlier) in order to plan robbing them, the bed he sleeps in "turned out to be a diabolical instrument of torture. Several hours of wriggling and twitching convinced me that the mattress design had been borrowed from some old handbook of the Spanish Inquisition" (102). After he breaks into the Ramsay house, he finds himself

> in a tiny chapel . . . Devoid of windows, low-ceilinged, stifling—the place might have been a sepulchre in a

---

it. Some words he pronounced like an Englishman while others were tinged by the modulations of the Romance tongues and still others—those that contained fricatives—had a curiously Slavic sound. There were even a few melodic intonations reminiscent of Chinese" (22).

> catacomb. And the old guy on the altar didn't enliven it much, either, because his expression was as grim as a Baptist preacher's in Las Vegas on New Year's Eve. I had a spooky feeling he actually sensed what I was up to.
>
> Shaking off these silly fancies, however, I again set my mind to business. Beside me, mounted on the wall, was a superb polychromed wooden crucifix. In the dancing candlelight, the flesh of Jesus looked as real as my own. (128)

Unwilling to read these and other signs (he's already stolen one crucifix), Arnold visits the Devil again in hopes of getting more money out of him by telling him that Hopkins isn't his real name, that the contract he signed isn't legal.

> The Devil looked perplexed. He ran the tips of his fingers over his hair, which was so dark, glistening and plastered down that it scarcely seemed like hair at all. Rather, it appeared as if someone had painted his skull with black enamel. Sunlight from the windows glanced off its smooth surface, creating a dazzling halo above his crown. (143)[20]

Arnold wants to renegotiate the contract—$2000 for the soul, he argues, is a little cheap—but the Devil is not deceived.

> "Do you really hope to hoodwink the Devil?" he went on in a voice as shrill as a fire siren. "You wish to cheat and hornswoggle the Prince of Darkness? Simpleton! Dimwitted dreamer! Wretched imbecile! . . . You signed the agreement and accepted the money. Now you are jolly

20 The Devil himself is described here by Hopkins as an artifact, an antique worth possessing.

> well mine—flesh, blood, bone and spirit. You're doomed... doomed! My mark is on you. You're the Devil's creature—his puppet, his little mechanical toy." (145)

At some point, as they become more and more enmeshed in events beyond their control, Greenan's characters are made to sense that some unseen hand is at work manipulating their lives. In *Heart of Gold*, for example, Reverend Lenox mistakenly thinks: "It was almost as if a divine hand were protecting him" (234). In *The Bric-a-Brac Man* Arnold Hopkins

> wondered why I was being confronted by these crazy situations. My life was nothing but dilemmas. Why couldn't straightforward commercial activities remain straightforward commercial activities? Why did customers drop dead at the wheel of their car owing me money? Why did old ladies with marquetry chairs turn out be swindlers? Why did victims wake up during burglaries? Why did Greek landlords lose their checkbooks when it was time to settle bills? It was almost as if a wicked bewitcher had slapped the evil eye on me. (108)

One senses this "wicked bewitcher" at work as Arnold's frustration and bad luck increase, e.g. when everyone in line to pay their bill at the restaurant needs change and Arnold has to watch while the furniture is driven off by Tyrone Crabtree. Scenes such as this and others are not unlike the "absurd builders" (179) who put up a fence that blocks Humbert Humbert's view of nymphets at play in the school yard outside his window. For in a large sense Arnold is trapped in a typical Greenan novel, complete with his trademark eccentrics, old comedians who tell incessantly their bad jokes (Barney Slocum's father, Lew Slocum), and murder. He's also caught in the Greenan paradigm of encounter/bad luck/farce/nightmare/beyond. Arnold's encounter, however, with someone who says he's the Devil, puts his fate firmly in theological as well as auctorial hands. Alfred Omega, as the narrator of *It Happened in Boston?* mad though he perhaps is, may be Greenan's most self-aware character when he says "God and (I have good reason to believe) the Devil are pursuing me" (276).

How aware is Hopkins that his crimes might constitute offenses to the Divine? Not very. After all, he began committing them long before Barney Slocum offered him money to steal a crucifix and long before he sells his soul to Senor Felix Jerónimo Rodríguez Diego de Merendaro y Alcalá. He has, for example, when he was married and broke, stolen urns from a cemetery. "[S]urely I needed those urns more than the man who was lying underneath them. Ethics, while wonderful, are only an abstraction" (120). On the metaphysical level the essential Greenan question, as articulated by Arnold, may be "Had I imagined these things? Was I living in the real world or had I plunged into some psychotic delusion?" (192). On the theological level it may be the same question the Devil asks him: "Do you believe in original sin?" How a character answers that question, as in Flannery O'Connor's Gothic-tinged tales, can determine his fate.

Arnold isn't the sociopathic murderer that Reverend Lenox is, nor is he a brain-damaged murderer like Algernon Pendleton. That people die around him, sometimes because of his actions (posing as Hogan Guilfoyle, for example), makes him ill. "The Ramsay girl, and now Hogan. I was going through life like the Black Plague," he thinks. "My stomach began to churn. I ran into the bathroom and was sick" (160). Which makes the "happy ending" of *The Bric-a-Brac Man* all the more troubling. Elements of the plot come clear to Hopkins as the novel progresses. When, for example, Tyrone catches up with him, he realizes that the Frankenstein figure described by Guilfoyle is the same man who killed him. "Pieces of an appalling mosaic commenced to click into place in my agitated mind. I grew limp with terror" (158). And with Barney Slocum's help he learns that his cousin Maurice and the Ramsay sister who lured Arnold into her arms conspired to set Arnold up as the murderer of the other two sisters. But, as with Greenan's other protagonists (from Alfred Omega in his first novel to Mickey Schreiner in *Dread of Night*), Arnold Hopkins does not see the deeper pattern behind these machinations. "I sensed a pattern of mad logic to these events, though try as I might, I couldn't bring it into focus" (192).

When Maurice dies along with Tyrone Crabtree in a fall from Hopkins's building and Maurice is mistaken for Arnold, Barney Slocum suggests that he take on his cousin's identity. Maurice is wealthier, yes, but he's also, as it has turned out, even more of a sinner (with murder on his list of deeds) than Arnold. The imposture works, perhaps all too well. "There have been moments when I actually felt I was Maurice Fitzjames—peculiar as that may sound" (209–10).

And what of the Devil? Earlier, the Devil's servant, Xochimilco, tells Arnold that his boss has been put away in a sanitarium and relates Merendaro's history, about how his father tossed him out the window onto a fire (continuing the defenestration theme) and at that point he thought of himself as the Devil whom God had thrown out of heaven. But since then Arnold believes he's seen the two of them again.

> Is the Devil really the Devil? I wonder. Hogan Guilfoyle signed a contract with him, and not long after, he died. Then I signed one, and what happened? I was shot at, almost thrown off a roof, and narrowly missed being burned alive. Yes—and Maurice, my double, was killed. (210)

Perhaps, Arnold thinks, "one day I'll come across a Jonathan Wild tea towel—the rarest and most precious kind—and the Devil and I can negotiate a whole new deal" (211). Whether Hopkins is deluded or not, sane or insane, the thought of his embodying the persona of his cousin Maurice and renegotiating with the Devil is hardly comforting.

CHAPTER SIX

"A PRETTY GLOOMY IDEA": THE TRICKSTER FIGURE IN *KEEPERS* (1978)

I. *"All profundities are pitfalls"*

Keepers features Greenan's smallest cast of characters and, next to *Nightmare*, his simplest plot. On Scarp Island two nurses, a young woman, Adriana Danziger, and a young man, newly hired Edward (Ned) Osgood, watch over a murderer/madman Nigel Vaughan, brother of a Rhode Island politician Richard Vaughan. The lunatic is held in West Cottage, and up the hill the politician stays part-time with Nigel's wife Elisabeth at Grayhaven, the mainhouse on "the brow of the hill." Grayhaven is "a bulky, fourteen-room structure of fieldstone, flanked by numerous sheds and outbuildings that had long since been bleached to a uniform sickly pallor by the sea wind and the salt spray" (7). That "brow" and "sickly pallor" identify the house and the setting with the familiar (Hawthorne, Poe) Gothic building and trope of the house as body, where the sickness of the one fuses with the other. The Vaughan brothers' father was also a politician, more powerful than his politician son and equally corrupt.[21]

21 Greenan will play out the theme of politics and corruption to greater effect in his next novel *A Can of Worms*, and extend it into the realm of homegrown terrorists in *La nuit du jugement/Doomsnight* and *Dread of Night*.

Unlike in his preceding novels, there is no protagonist, though there is a character, Nigel Vaughan, around whom the other characters and the action revolves. Early in the novel Greenan links the brothers Vaughan by having them express the same idea, though the meaning behind the ideas are distinctly different. "All profundities are pitfalls, I suspect," Nigel wisely says (21), and nine pages later his brother Richard, speaking of Nigel's reading habits, will say, less wisely, "The voices of those great authors combined in a siren song that lured my poor brother to disaster. Profound ideas can be treacherous" (30). These two brothers, a madman and a politician, share more than similar thoughts and a genetic and mythic (Cain and Abel) ancestry: Nigel's wife (estranged, of course, since Nigel is a murderer and behind bars, albeit not institutional ones) happens also to be her brother-in-law's mistress. Richard, the corrupt politician whose murder the mad Nigel will plot, describes to Edward Osgood, his distant nephew hired as his brother's new keeper, what it's like to look after a brother who is a homicidal maniac:

> "Edward, you have no idea. Still, one can't shirk one's duties," the politician answered patly, smoke wreathing the crown of his head like a halo. "The worst of it is, people inevitably feel guilty when a member of their family is mentally ill . . . You keep recalling the past, searching for the root of the tragedy. You delve and brood. You endlessly analyze. Old, old scenes in old, old settings haunt you like specters from the grave . . . We're both of us locked up in a moldy labyrinth of bitter memories." (28)

In the novel's character constellation that functions in place of a protagonist, Nigel is also paired with Ned Osgood, himself a deceiver and murderer, though the relationship between Ned and Nigel is more one of a petty thief to a master criminal, a poor deceiver to a true trickster. Osgood—the male romantic interest, if this were, say, a typical entertainment, rather than a novel by Greenan—does not live up to his name. In fact, he already has a past as a thief and abuser of women. His first sexual encounter with the lonely Adriana is, in fact, a rape, though it will take Adriana a while to recognize it as such. "How many women have you treated that way, Edward?" she asks him. "He almost smiled. 'Most girls aren't so hard to get along with,' he answered, sidestepping the question" (44). After Nigel informs him about a safe in his brother's house, Osgood's avarice is pricked. Then, caught in the act of opening the safe, he kills Louise Vaughan accidentally. "Suddenly it dawned on him that he was supporting the woman's whole weight. Looking down he could see her two small feet in their coral slippers dangling several inches above the floor" (76). When he sets her down, "her blonde head drooped onto her shoulder like the head of an unstrung marionette" (77). Osgood takes the corpse to West Cottage and places it outside Nigel's cell, but is seen doing this by Adriana. From this point, the lunatic's goals will be threefold: to see that his brother is killed, that Osgood is blamed for the death, and that he escapes from his confinement.

Adriana Danziger, the novel's only sympathetic figure besides Nigel, provides the lunatic with the means (a key) to effect his goals. Nigel, who hears Adriana cry the night she is raped and says the two of them are like brother and sister, will become her avenging angel, and she in turn will help him escape.

Richard Vaughan, Edward Osgood, Adriana Danziger—all three of them are paired with Nigel and it is he who will control their fates. Though the novel is told in third person omniscient, the world of *Keepers* centers on a psychopath and murderer, one with whom Greenan allows the reader once again to sympathize.

> "Faced with prolonged misery and certain death, the so-called normal man has a desperate need of tricks and stratagems if he wishes to go on living," said Nigel, as he cut his fingernails with a clipper. "Confronted with the stark horror of reality, the sane person requires all manner of illusions—defense mechanisms, they're aptly termed—in order to survive, for without these self-deceptions he would have motivation for nothing but suicide."
>
> "A pretty gloomy idea," Osgood commented indifferently.
>
> "I'll say it is—yet true nonetheless. I helped a man commit suicide at Rose Hill Manor, years ago. Showed him how to tear his shirt-sleeves off and twist them into a noose. There was a great furor when they found him hanging from a pipe in the bathroom . . . So when psychiatrists contend that madmen lose touch with reality, the good doctors are deluding themselves. It's the sane who dwell in a fantasy world, and the insane who see things as they actually are. That's why they go crazy."
>
> Nigel carefully clipped the nail on his thumb, cutting it almost to the quick.
>
> Osgood said, "I've been wondering about the safe up at Grayhaven . . ." (58–59)

Who and what is this character who in his madness makes so much sense? Nigel's logic is irresistible, much more so than a sociopath like Nick Corey's in Jim Thompson's *Pop. 1280.*

Thompson's homicidal sheriff experiences an emptiness (a kind of weepy-eyed, comic existentialism) from which "all the sad terrible things" derive.

> There were the helpless little girls cryin' when their own daddies crawled into bed with 'em. There were the men beating their wives, the women screamin' for mercy. There were the kids wettin' in the beds from fear and nervousness, and their mothers dosin' 'em with red pepper for punishment. There were the haggard faces, drained white from hookworm and blotched with scurvy. There was the near-starvation, the never-bein'-full, the debts that always outrun the credits. There was the how-we-gonna-eat, how-we-gonna-sleep, how-we-gonna-cover-poor-bare-asses thinkin'. The kind of thinkin' that when you ain't doing nothing else but that, why you're better off dead. Because that's the emptiness thinkin' and you're already dead inside, and all you'll do is spread the stink and the terror, the weepin' and wailin', the torture, the starvation, the shame of your deadness. Your emptiness. (*Pop. 1280* 198)

Both characters, Nick and Nigel, are full of "tricks and stratagems" to overcome "the stark horror of reality," but in his erudition and theatricality, his childishness and beguiling charm, Nigel sets himself apart from the psychopaths in the novels of Thompson. To survive the Emptiness, Nick Corey develops the delusion that he's Jesus Christ put on earth "for the miracle of promotin' people to glory" (210) by killing them. Steadfast in his madness, Nigel has no need for such delusions. His patter is a barrage of ingenuous sense and nonsense, spiked with word play, historical and literary anecdotes, and the mundane.

> "Ah, Albert [a policemen hitting up on Adriana]—you're a smooth operator," Nigel remarked with a leer. "Smooth as silk. But beware—one of your colleagues might have to arrest you for stealing hearts, and you'll land in jail. Ha, ha. Did you know Cardinal Richelieu had an enemy of his locked up for sixty years? Sixty! In a dungeon of the Bastille on a lettre de cachet. And prisons are such depressing places. No offense, Albert. Wasn't that vicious of the Cardinal? Wasn't it, Adriana? How would you like to spend a lifetime behind bars? Or even half a lifetime? You wouldn't, I'm sure—and I don't blame you . . . Well, I'm relieved to know everything is going to be all right again. There are more ways to kill a dog than by choking him with butter, eh? I only wish Albert would invite me to Luna Disco. I wouldn't refuse. Ha, ha. I'd go in a minute. Yes, I'd raise Cain, if I were able—though I wouldn't raise Abel, if I were Cain." (184–85)

In that revealing, chiastic allusion (Cain/able—Abel/Cain) which the cop can't catch, Nigel's audacity and wit become perversely admirable.

It's not a question of our identifying with the madman; Nigel is too much the lunatic for us to do that. But with the death of his wife Louise, Nigel becomes increasingly sympathetic. This puts the reader once again on a slippery slope, feeling sympathy for a murderous psychopath. Unlike Reverend Lenox and Arnold Hopkins, but like Algernon Pendleton, Nigel's madness and acts of retribution free him of our moral condemnation. That Osgood will kill himself in the manner (shirtsleeve for noose) prescribed by Nigel to a fellow inmate is this avenging angel's crowning touch. In the end, posing as a doctor, he escapes from his new institution. "A month later, when Adriana made her promised visit, Nigel was still at large" (197).

Nigel resembles less one of Greenan's confidence men (Reverend Lenox and Arnold Hopkins) than he does the figure of the Trickster, as described in Warwick Wadlington's *The Confidence Game in American Literature*:

> The Trickster, . . . straddling oppositions, embodies two antithetical, nonrational experiences of man with the natural world, his society, and his own psyche: on the one hand, a force of treacherous disorder that outrages and disrupts, and on the other hand, an unanticipated, usually unintentional benevolence in which trickery is at the expense of inimical forces and for the benefit of mankind. Operating at those extremes of human experience that are almost impossible to recognize outside fictions and intellectually puzzling within them, the Trickster may appear as an anarchic creature, at once transhuman, transanimal, and transdeific, who seeks self-gratification by japes played at the level of the insane or the infantile, yet whose unaltruistic appetites establish social order and create its elemental instruments. (15–16)

As a psychotic murderer willing to kill anyone, Nigel is a lord of disorder; by effecting the deaths of his brother and Osgood, he rights the judicial scales. Infantile and insane, his madness is yet a form of sanity. Standing outside the circle of humanity, he is more human than those within it. According to Jung, the trickster figure "is a forerunner of the savior, and, like him, god, man, and animal at once. He is both subhuman and superhuman, a bestial and divine being, whose chief and most alarming characteristic is his unconsciousness" (143).[22] That we can't tell what is a psychotic's lucky guess at the nature of things and what a sane man's reasoning makes it impossible for us to separate Nigel's consciousness from his unconsciousness. If profundities are indeed pitfalls, as this loony says, they are nonetheless profound. "One wretched, petty, paltry slip and you go sailing off to limbo like a thing on wires" (183–84), Nigel tells Adriana, effectively describing man's condition in a mechanistic universe. "You people kept telling me Nigel was an idiot when I was out to Scarp—but he isn't, is he?" asks Raymond Calderone, the detective investigating the case. "He has his good days and bad days," Adriana responds "noncommittally" (185).

II. *"Perhaps there really is a righteous God"*

Richard Rorty, in his otherwise perceptive essay *The Barber of Kasbeam: Nabokov on Cruelty*, claims that Humbert and Kinbote are "exactly as good a writer, exactly as much of an

22 "If we consider, for example, the daemonic features exhibited by Yahweh in the Old Testament, we shall find in them not a few reminders of the unpredictable behavior of the trickster, of his senseless orgies of destruction and his self-imposed sufferings, together with the same gradual development into a savior and his simultaneous humanization" (Jung 136). The Deity as Trickster, as the Lord of Dupery, is central to Alfred Omega's theology in *It Happened in Boston?*

artist, capable of creating exactly as much iridescent ecstasy, as Nabokov himself" (24). Rorty's mistake here is, in part, to subtract morality from ecstasy and art, ethics from aesthetics, whereas for Nabokov at least half of art's four principle characteristics ("curiosity, tenderness, kindness, ecstasy" [*Lolita*, "On A Book Entitled *Lolita*," p. 317]) have an ethical base. It's equally important in reading Greenan not to give his trickster characters the upper hand. Nigel Vaughan's wit and ability to manipulate the plot does not make him his author's artistic equal any more than are Greenan's ethically challenged first person narrators (Arnold Hopkins, Algernon Pendleton, Steven Pierglass, Alfred Omega) or his other inventive third person sociopaths (Rev. Lenox, Betsy March). The created can never be on equal terms with the creator; the character is always within and never outside the master's plan. "*[W]here there is a work of art, there is no madness*" (Foucault, *Madness and Civilization*, 289; his italics). All the more reason, then, for us not to fall completely for Nigel's patter, lest we sail off "like a thing on wires" manipulated by the trickster.

The attentive reader, at the end of *Keepers*, will hear in the clink and final clank a perfection of plot ("The plots of God are perfect" [Poe, *Eureka* 164]), surely attributable to the mortal hand of the author more than that of his character. The plot of *Keepers* involves a potentially incriminating duplicate key which Nigel gets rid of by means of three balloons he's talked Adriana into bringing him. With this duplicate key, the novel's narrative mechanism locks into place as solidly as Shadmeister's G.A.B.A. at the end of *Nightmare*. This interlocking of the elements of plot reveals the author's hand as much as it underscores the mechanistic universe.

A tableau of Nigel in his cell watching Edward beat Adriana can serve, in its stage-bound formality, as an instance of authorial inscription.

> "You're crazy," she said huskily. "You're dangerous. A psychopath. I should have known that first night—should have realized when you killed . . ."
>
> "Shut up!" the youth bellowed, raising his fist again and taking another stride in her direction . . .
>
> For the next minute or two, the three of them seemed deprived of all capacity to move. Like wax figures in a chamber of horrors, they stood congealed in their dramatic poses. (144)

The distancing effect of the tableau's artifice (wax figures/chamber of horrors/congealed dramatic poses) at this dramatic, truth-telling moment in the plot, allows us to ponder for a moment the smaller mechanisms at work in the novel. For example, we can follow the adventure of motifs as they grow outward, like Nigel in the end "at large" in the world, like the madness that is spreading: *crazy - dangerous - psychopath - murderer* ("you killed"). Or we can follow the dialectic in the tableau—the victim (Adriana), the perpetrator (Ned Osgood) observed (though not from his point of view, the POV is high angle omniscient) by a madman (Nigel), part avenging angel, part (or whole?) pure psychotic, as if Nigel's psychosis has reached the point where goodness and evil mingle ("he has his good days and his bad days"). "Nigel staring wide-eyed through the bars of his prison, Adriana cringing on the rug as tears flowed down her cheeks, and the grim wrathful Osgood with his hand clenched into a huge knot of whitened knuckles ready to strike again" (144). On an even more micro-structural level, we can follow the dialectical spiral of the tableau with a simple 1-2-3 numbering ("minute [1] or two [2], the three of them [3]"), until stasis is reached, though the elements in the picture keep the mind in motion (narratively, thematically, aesthetically) long enough for the plot and the actors to kick in again, for the mechanism to unfreeze. "Then the deathlike hush was broken by the chiming bell of the nearby buoy, and the youth lowered his arm, snarled an obscenity, turned on his heels, and walked swiftly from the corridor" (144).

"Perhaps there really is a righteous God," thinks Nigel when Adriana innocently leaves "the ornate key" on the desk in the passageway that leads to Nigel's cell (165), allowing Nigel to maneuver the key into his hands and put his plans into effect. Of course Adriana misses the signs laid in her path that would reveal how Nigel managed to leave his cell without anyone knowing it (the key, the balloons) as she gazes for the last time "over all the familiar features of the small crescent cove," where her romance with Ned Osgood began.

> "Why did it happen?" she asked softly.
>
> At the tip of the crescent's southern cusp two plovers strutted on spindly yellow legs along the shore, their sun-bleached beige bodies almost invisible against the background of sand.
>
> "Why did it happen?" she repeated, a note of anger in her voice.
>
> Around the narrow headland an outboard motorboat sped, trailing a lacy wake like a bridle train. The roar of

> its engine startled her, while the plovers immediately flapped their wings and flew up into the sky, showing their black-spotted tails and whistling plaintively.
>
> Turning, she went back the way she had come. The sun was bright, yet she felt oddly chilled. (193–94)

The two plovers, in their near-invisibility ("almost invisible against the background") and non-airborne condition, are insufficient as clues. Now with "anger in her voice," as if frustrated with fate's opacity, she asks again, this time to have the wake of a motorboat compared to a bridle train, a rather cruel simile considering that she had expected to marry Osgood, and then for the plovers to take flight, as if asking her to look at their black-spotted tails, to listen to their plaintive song, as if they were the clue she needed. Instead, she turns away, notes the bright sun, feels "oddly chilled," but misses this last clue in the sequence that runs 1) hidden-in-the-background, 2) up-in-the-air, 3) sun suggests balloon. It's as if the text wanted to speak to its characters, but can't, not really, it's not allowed, at least not by this author.

Two pages later, after she's been questioned by Calderone about the duplicate key, and is on the boat leaving the island, she realizes, but doesn't tell the detective, how Nigel used the balloons she gave him to dispose of the key.

> As they chugged away from the jetty, she glanced back at the white-brick cottage with its terra-cotta tiled roof. Automatically her eyes were drawn to Nigel's living room window, and she suddenly realized how he had gotten rid of the second key. Yes, she thought, of course! He tied

> it to the balloons. He tied it to the three orange balloons, and let the wind carry it out to sea. A brief, joyless laugh broke from her lips. (196)

By eliciting our sympathy for Nigel and by masterminding a plot beyond the mind of his madman, Greenan is the trickster of whom we should most be wary.

CHAPTER SEVEN

A BUCKET OF MAGGOTS, *A CAN OF WORMS* (1987): METHODS OF ORDER IN GREENAN'S MACABRE COLLAGE

Mimes, in the form of God on high,
Mutter and mumble low,
And hither and thither fly—
Mere puppets they, who come and go . . .
But see, amid the mimic rout
A crawling shape intrude!
A blood-red thing that writhes from out
The scenic solitude!
It writhes!—it writhes!—with mortal pangs
The mimes become its food,
And the angels sob at vermin fangs
In human gore imbued.

—"The Conqueror Worm," Edgar Allan Poe

Like a vision out of Poe or Goya, *A Can of Worms* (1987) wriggles into view. Puppets of greed, marionettes with limited views, the comic, the psychotic, the cheaters and the cheated, the unfortunately fated, the dying mistaken for the dead. Greenan's last novel to be published in English before the appearance of *Dread of Night* in late 2009, is, among others things, another marvel of formal control. No single character serves to center the novel, only a chain of circumstances that sprout from the death of Ludy Gilman, a night clerk at "the Montevideo Motel on Route 3A outside Nashua, New Hampshire," who collapses from a coronary thrombosis while telling a sex joke to two maids. The maids "at first thought he was just kidding around. Ludy liked nothing better than a little slapstick-pratfall comedy" (1). The events that reverberate from this pratfall into death form the novel's squirming plot. The plot really is a can of worms, in all its reflexive and thematic referentiality and fleshy reality. Above all, the conceit allows us to experience *A Can of Worms* as a poem, a sorrowful, macabre collage framed by two scenes at the Montevideo Motel.

Within this frame *A Can of Worms* describes a Boston littered with various drunks, in particular a wino named Whitey Frainer; a corrupt Boston politician, Phil Delaunay; his psychotically sexed sister Melissa (Missy); her sadistic sometimes lover and hitman Stanley Gloag; a lawyer who is also an extortionist, Ludy Gilman's brother Harold; a dumb but loyal Irish cop, Kevin Reedy, who has violent reveries and is in Delaunay's pocket; another cop, Frankie Gates, in love with Harold Gilman's rich realtor wife Magda; petty thieves like Ossie Peña, a dope-smoking attendant at Suds for Duds; a black pimp, Scipio Africanus; a blackmailing private eye, Fritz Pomerantz. Add a couple of severed heads and Boston's racism, as well as assorted sins and crimes, such as adultery, murder, and incest, and you have the mix that makes for *A Can of Worms*. Phil Delaunay puts it like this: "Instead of concentrating on rustling up support for the nomination, I'm dithering around with a personal problem. My head is crammed with garbage—extortion demands, secret payoffs, criminals, dead bodies, police investigations" (126). Garbage and dead bodies, as we all know, breed lots of worms.

Greenan's plot is an elaborate weave of mostly malign purposes, missed connections, dead souls—all made palpable with sensual and symbolic specificity. Take any strand, pull on it, the Peña plot thread, for example, and everything squirms. One night Ossie Peña looks out of the barred window at the back of the Suds for Duds laundromat and sees in the parking lot a man and woman in a new Audi talking and then the woman shooting the man. "[L]ike a magician performing a bit of hocus-pocus, she brought forth a small gun, pointed it at the man's chest, and shot him. Two infinitesimal tongues of flame licked the weapon's muzzle, while the double recoil sent a tremor up her extended arm" (38). Peña, after the woman leaves, will steal the stereo from the Audi and refuse to help the man who is still alive. Without his knowing it, he has witnessed Missy's attempted murder of her blackmailer Harold Gilman, who had found in a trunk a batch of overhead shots taken by his late brother of couples in bed at the Montevideo Motel. Peña's theft will end up getting him killed by the cop loyal to the Delaunay family, Kevin Reedy. Gilman's disappearance will lead Magda Gilman to hire a private detective Fritz Pomerantz who will be killed by Missy's hitman companion Stanley Gloag after Fritz has been ripped off by the pimp Scipio Africanus in their scheme to blackmail Missy. Gloag will be killed by Magda's lover, Boston detective Frankie Gates, when Gloag tries to eliminate Magda Gilman, whom Missy mistakenly thinks is behind the blackmail. Gates will be too late to save Magda from Kevin Reedy, who (too late) will learn that the photos contain not only pictures of his friend Phil Delaunay and Missy in bed together, but also Reedy's love Rita, dead in a traffic accident after her final tryst with Delaunay.

How tightly packed the worms are in Greenan's plot. But what would the container be without a texture to fill it? Again, consider the minor figure of Ossie Peña and his surrounds, as Greenan introduces them in Chapter 7 (of 44):

> Shortly before twelve that same night the last customer, a demented old man in a red-checked hat with elephantine earflaps left the Suds for Duds Laundromat carrying his well-worn clothing, still hot from the dryer, in a wrinkled plastic garbage bag.
>
> "Every day we get more and more of those deinstitutionalized characters in this dump," Ossie Peña soliloquized, watching him shamble down the street.
>
> Then the attendant locked and bolted the front door, rolled all the hampers beneath the long Formica tables, switched off the lights, and went back through the shadows to the cubbyhole that served as an office. From around his scrawny neck he took the earphones of his Walkman WM-7 and adjusted them to his head, after which he splashed another generous dose of Bardolino into the chipped teacup, recapped the half-gallon jug, and lit up a *porra*. (35)

Perhaps one can hear in "a wrinkled plastic garbage bag," "dump," "cubbyhole," and "scrawny neck" the distant melody of worms, as one can in this youth's "curly black hair" (more on the use of hair to suggest worms in a moment), but a louder echo awaits us when we recall the "still hot from the dryer" as we read a hundred pages later of Reedy's putting Peña in one of the laundromat's dryers and leaving him there until he's dead. "Get the fuck in there, you maggot," Reedy tells Peña before tossing him into the dryer. "The shape of the drum forced him into a fetal position" (141). Thus begins the two-page-long birth of Ossie Peña's death. Surprised that "the little hump" is dead, Reedy lifts "one of Peña's eyelids" to make sure. "What he saw shocked him. The pupil was hardly bigger than a pinhead, while all the rest of the eye had turned an ocherous brown. The whole orb had shrunk and shriveled, so that it now appeared grotesquely small for its socket" (144).

(Such Grand Guignol descriptions, as we've by now amply seen, are part of this master's repertoire, where the specificity of detail and sound—e.g, the *o*, *r*, and *k* sounds in *ocherous brown / whole orb / shrunk / grotesquely / socket* sequence above—impresses the scene's horror upon our consciousness, while at the same time imbedding deeper the novel's darker themes, made none the lighter, of course, by the scene's aesthetic properties.)

The Walkman Peña adjusts to his head when we first meet him (Peña is a John Coltrane fan) also has a physical and symbolic role to play in the life and death of this minor character. Affected by the sight of the apparently dead Gilman in the Audi, Peña crosses himself before going to work. But when he tries to lift Gilman's wrist watch, Gilman clutches him. Peña "with a jerk liberated his hand from the macabre grip. Through the open door he backed, but to his horror something grabbed him by the nape of the neck and prevented his retreat. He let out a yelp and wriggled like a belly dancer . . . The Walkman wire had tangled itself around the car's shift, and it was the metal band of his headphones that had clutched him by the throat" (40). The Walkman as a lifeline, a *conscience*-line, trying to hold him back from a crime far worse than theft. "'Aagh! The guy's still alive,' he wailed, his hundred-pound body shaking convulsively. '*Por Dios!* He ain't dead. Holy shit! Did he see my face? *Hombre*, I got to get the hell out of here' " (41). Only to be tumbled and "roasted alive" (141) later in the "sulfurous glow" of the laundromat for his sin, although he "finger[ed] the black wire of his Walkman as though he were telling the beads of a rosary" (139).

Above all the novel's texture is established, as is almost everything in this vermiculate tale, by the image of worms—worms directly referenced, alluded to, loomed into verbs, metaphors, symbols, a Weltanschauung, a controlling conceit. The title Greenan places in the mouth of Melissa Delaunay's psychotic equal, Stanley Gloag: "Well, it's interesting—this blackmailing business. Better handle it right, or you'll be opening a can of worms" (35). And out of this can Greenan's characters avariciously crawl. "Everybody's into moral turpitude, these days" (7), thinks Harold Gilman when he looks at his brother's candid overhead shots of a "cast of characters . . . old and ugly or fat and homely—much more comic than sexy" (6) and comes across Phil Delaunay and his sister Missy "going at it like a couple of alley cats. The dirty bastards" (7). Human bodies, naked or not, root and wriggle throughout the novel. Listening to Magda Gilman tell of how her college friend, the politically empowered Missy Delaunay, took Magda's first husband from her, Frankie Gates is reminded of "a gruff pronouncement his Uncle Dinny had once delivered when he'd heard of an unmarried girl's pregnancy. 'They *will* fuck,' the old donkey had muttered sagely. Sensing that this was the wrong occasion for telling such an anecdote, the reclining detective kept silent" (26).

Reedy recalls Missy as a teenager when she "just kept on rubbing her ass or her pointy little tits on any healthy-looking male who happened to visit the house," no matter the number of psychiatrists her politico dad, Sunny Ned Delaunay, sent her to. "Memories of those days stirred in Reedy's mind like maggots" (46). Crashing for a night after trying to protect Phil and Missy, Reedy dreams of Rita. "But just as he was about to caress the alluring woman, something hot and moist wriggled into his ear"—Missy's tongue. "Giggling, the woman slithered off his body" (63). Sick with a cold after killing and decapitating Harold Gilman, Reedy lies in bed, "his hands . . . wriggling on the counterpane" (82). Magda, unable to give Frankie Gates a straight answer to his marriage proposal, "wriggled in the chair, and the green silk of her loose gown rippled sinuously" (182). Driving Magda to his property under construction near the Fens (a gift from Phil Delaunay) and to her death, Reedy "skillfully wormed his way through to Boylston Street" (198). Fighting Frankie Gates after killing and decapitating Magda, Reedy "wriggled loose" (206). Ossie Peña, who "wriggled like a belly dancer," also is shown "wriggling" into his jeans (92) and heard swearing "devoutly as he wiggled his tiny foot into a wing-tipped loafer that had a two-inch stacked heel" (95). Ludy's hair is wavy, Peña's curly, Melissa's ropy. "[A] sudden gust of wind wrapped spirals of yellow hair around her pouting mouth" (112).

Worms, maggots, creatures that live underground or off the dead. Phil Delaunay tells his loyal but dumb Irish cop and boyhood friend Kevin Reedy, "The whole wretched business is turning into a rat's nest" (125). For Magda, thinking about her avaricious relatives eager to inherit her fortune, "Human beings are vultures" (145). "Ain't no shortage of men in the world," says Scipio's prostitute Rubyjewel. "Why, you keep running into them everyplace you go—like cockroaches" (97).

The apotheosis of the worm conceit occurs when Frankie Gates is called to the apartment of Lily Spritzer who has reported that the bums fighting in her alley ("the whole assembly collapsed on the littered asphalt in a wriggling tangle of arms, heads, and legs") have broken into her house and robbed her.

> Lily Spritzer thanked him for coming, showed him to the door, and returned to the window to watch the comedy.
>
> Reaching the alley by means of the cellar exit, he found the battle proceeding at a fast and furious clip. Grunts and curses filled the air, and now and then a bleary-eyed face, unshaven and wine-red in color, would stare out from the knot of writhing bodies.
>
> "Break it up, you fucking grease bags. This isn't the Boston Garden," the detective snarled, kicking a broad rump in dirty denim which projected from the slithering heaving huddle.
>
> The recipient of this boot, a roly-poly vagabond, tore himself from the melee, and giving Gates a why-don't-you-mind-your-own-business glare, waddled off in the direction of the street. The other combatants paid him no heed, however, and he was obliged to kick several more backsides before the lacework of thrashing limbs finally unraveled and the scrimmage came to its inconclusive and inglorious end. (161)

From out of this "knot of writhing bodies" might have crawled a somewhat different worm, Whitey Frainer, no less a bum, but capable, almost in spite of himself, of a deed disconnected from the world's great motivators: fear and greed. It is Whitey who looks through "the gaping hole in the middle of the landing, where the renovators had ripped out the staircase to the ground floor" (52) of Reedy's house (another of Greenan's gothic structures) near the Fens and, in hopes of stealing money, looks into "a bulging plastic shopping bag" and sees "or, at least, imagined that he saw— . . . an elaborate Halloween mask, a rubbery horror complete with livid complexion, gore-stained lips and teeth, and jagged glistening neck wound" (54).

> But though he was frightened, he was entranced as well, and continued to gaze into the dead eyes long after his brain had advised him to flee. All this vibration soon had an effect on the object he held, for the detached head, as if wishing to avoid his concentrated scrutiny, at last tumbled over on its sallow cheek. When that occurred, two amputated hands appeared beneath it in a carmine pool of blood. (54)

Reedy returns and throws the head of Harold Gilman in his burning fireplace. From his vantage point on the second floor, Whitey Frainer looks on. "An incandescent gold ring circled the head, which lay facedown on the burning paper. From the wavy hair tendrils of gray smoke seeped, and slowly meandered up the chimney." Readers of Greenan's first novel *It Happened in Boston?* will now have journeyed from the possibly illusory crown placed on the head of that novel's narrator, Alfred Omega, at book's end to this fiery temporal halo above the decapitated head of Harold Gilman. Then the head falls and rolls out of the fire.

> Frainer winced. Where the pale jowly face had been, there was now only a coarse mat of carbonized tissue and bone—a reeking black wound, devoid of human characteristics. Nothing remained but the teeth, and these were larger than they had been in life because the lips and gums were gone. From the smoldering skull, they shone with

> surprising brilliance, shone in a death smile full of mockery. (55)

The "lanky wino" later will have the opportunity to tell Frankie Gates about what he saw, but Frankie won't believe him until it's too late. Frankie, misreading the woman he loves, thinks Magda may have had her husband killed. By the time Frankie makes the connection between Reedy and the house near the Fens Whitey had told him about, Reedy has already decapitated Magda. The scene is replayed this time with Frankie watching his love's head burn in the fire.

> To view those so familiar features in such a setting—disembodied, surrounded by a corona of orange flame—almost made him doubt his sanity. And as he stared, even more bizarre things commenced to happen. Stirred by the fiery draft, the head's brown hair began drifting sinuously about her slightly flushed cheeks, while tiny wrinkles appeared at the corners of her mouth. Gradually the full lips parted. Between them he could see her white teeth. (203)

As Gates watches, further transformations occur to Magda's head, some of them, like the "tiny wrinkles" and sinuous hair and "tendrils of gray smoke" Whitey sees rising from Gilman's wavy hair, vermicular in shape.

> The heat of the blaze, the seething fluids and gases in the roasting skull, soon induced even more grotesque physiognomic changes. The pretty eyes took on a sly and evil look, and from one of them a gout of blood dribbled like

> a ruby tear. Swiftly the cheerful grin became a nasty simper, and the nose wrinkled up like an angry dog's. The floating hair caught fire, and in an instant became a glaring sunburst of yellow flame. Darkening to an umber hue, the skin cracked and shriveled, while an ear turned into a bit of twisted charcoal. (203)

Like an angel from above, Whitey throws down his "bottle of Cossack," saving Gates's life. "The detective [Reedy] with the revolver sighed wearily, and at almost the same instant, something extraordinary happened. A flashing, tumbling object of indeterminate size and shape came hurtling down from the upper reaches of the room, landed on the hearthstone like a grenade, and loudly shattered into a hundred scintillating fragments. An odor of alcohol pervaded the musty air" (205). Whitey tells Frankie that he was afraid Reedy "was going to shoot you and chop off your head" (207), but he makes the point several times that the vodka bottle was "nearly full," "brand new," "almost full."

A minor character or two is left standing or reeling at the novel's bleak end, but most everyone else is dead. The Gilman brothers—dead. Reedy kills himself but not before sending the compromising photos to the Massachusetts Coalition for Progress, and Missy is off to jail for shooting Harold Gilman. Ossie Peña, Stanley Gloag, Fritz Pomerantz, Magda Gilman—all dead. Only Frankie Gates is left standing in a state of ambiguity, "a tall uncertain figure starkly outlined against the dazzling white snow, . . . ponder[ing] the question of his guilt or innocence" (213).

There are no charming madmen or even a protagonist in *A Can of Worms*, just mainly a pervasive corruption—Boston by, say, Louis-Ferdinand Céline minus the ellipses. Ludy Gilman tells his joke about a woman who, after nine husbands, wanted to marry someone pure, a virgin, and finds one from the Australian Outback, who on their wedding night pushes all the furniture against the wall. "And the guy says, 'Well, my dear, I don't know much about ladies—but if they're anything like kangaroos, we'll need all the room we can get.'" But that's his last "dirty story" ("Nobody could tell a dirty story like Ludy Gilman"). "[H]e slumped to the nylon carpeted floor like a deflated balloon and, after a few feeble twitches, lay there perfectly still" (1). We can only find sex and race jokes in *A Can of Worms*. Irish cop to Armenian cop: "Hey, Aram! You ever hear that story about the cannibal butcher shop?" Armenian meat's the most expensive. Why? "And the butcher says, 'Lady, have you ever had to *clean* an Armenian?'" (190). Aram responds with the variation that Irish brains cost more. Why? "And the butcher says, 'Lady do you know how many Irishmen we have to kill to get a pound of brains?' " (191). One cop "with a brogue said plaintively, 'I didn't think that joke was so funny, Obie—did you?'" And the other Irish cop replies, "I thought it was in very bad taste—absolutely uncalled for. They're just not recruiting the same class of officers anymore. You can't walk into the station house these days without finding yourself ass-deep in vulgarity" (191). Ass deep we, too, are at the novel's end, ass deep in a universe as darkly comic as Jim Thompson's, albeit not as scatological.[23]

Such a vision of our species is not, of course, to every reader's liking. Christopher Lehmann-Haupt, for example, noted in his *New*

23 Two examples from Thompson's *Pop. 1280*: "when the ol' familiar taste of piss is back in your mouth, and you want to spit it out at everyone" (180); "you could make up poems about piss tinkling in pots and jaybirds with the bots and assholes tying knots and . . ." (184). A *bot* is a parasitical maggot, seen here in Thompson's image literally tying knots in anuses and figuratively as a marriage between the maggot and the flesh at the point of fecal excretion.

York Times review that whereas in his earlier novels, Greenan had "always succeeded at creating morally degenerate charmers, crazies whom one could root for because the moral universe they inhabited was ambiguous enough to make the intensity of their malevolent passions winning," in *A Can of Worms* he "keeps backing and filling, [as] a mean-spiritedness sets in that makes one wonder whether the joke is going to be worth one's trouble." Lehmann-Haupt's response suggests his praise for Greenan's previous novels was somewhat misconceived, not realizing that to be even a degree too charmed by his homicidal characters is to be implicated in their madness. The "backing and filling" the *Times* reviewer noted is more likely the worm-filled dirt falling on his own grave, unless we want to deny the likes of Swift, Twain, and Nathanael West their comic visions.

Yes, the human community in this and other Greenan works is a bucket of maggots, a can of worms. So much does this conceit invade every breath and page of the novel that readers like Lehmann-Haupt may find it, as Hawthorne said of his *Scarlet Letter*, "impossible to throw any cheering light" upon (qtd. in Kazin 31). Each time I read *A Can of Worms*, however, I can't help but be grateful for its humor and portrayal of its characters' predicaments and fates, and admire the aesthetic control the novel displays in its structure, language, motifs, rhythms, facticity, and plot. Nothing obliges the author of this entertaining but morally astringent comedy to be any more cheering than that.

Two brief scenes, as I mentioned in the beginning of this chapter, sturdily frame Greenan's entangled horrors. In the opening, Nathalie, a French-Canadian motel maid, sums up Ludy Gilman's death in an iambic dimeter French quatrain.

> While Arlene sobbed into a wad of pink Kleenex, Nathalie contemplated the faint impression in the nap of the electric-blue rug—the night manager's last at the Montevideo—and said in a tone of wonder, "So quick it happened. So sudden. Poor Ludy! He was not old, either. Only a touch of gray in his funny wavy hair. A crazy type, but I liked him—even if he was always pinching my *derrière* . . . and chasing after all the pretty young boys, too.
>
> "*La vie est brève,*
> *Un peu d'amour,*
> *Un peu de rève,*
> *Et puis, Bonjour.*"
>
> The brawny maid recited softly as though to herself. "But now, Arlene, it is necessary to dry your tears and call up Mr. Ortega. Tell him the whole tragic *histoire*. He will have to employ another night clerk *tout de suite*. And do not leave the desk until Alfred arrives, eh? There will be guests checking out. Me, I am going to poor Ludy's cabin and search for the names of his relatives. They will need to be phoned. It is all so sad and cruel." (2)

From a last "faint impression in the nap of the electric-blue rug" arises Greenan's wriggling tale, and on this same rug, as he closes the frame, the book will end.

> "Oh, *mon Dieu*—it's him, *absolument*," said Nathalie, jiggling her carpet sweeper. "The mouth, the eyes, the funny wavy hair—he is certainly the brother of Ludy who came here two months ago. Now he also is dead, and his rich wife, too—their heads chopped off like with the guillotine. *Quelle horreur!* . . . About faces, Mr. Ortega, I have

a memory *extraordinaire*. It is him," said the maid unequivocally. "And they are all of them dead—the two brothers and the young rich wife. What a tragedy, eh?" She struck a dramatic pose and recited feelingly:

"La vie est vaine,
Un peu d'espoir,
Un peu de haine,
Et puis, Bonsoir."

Mr. Ortega glanced at her quizzically, and said, "I don't speak French, Nathalie."

"*Quelle dommage*. That is a little poem by Alfred de Musset—a thing I learn when I am small at school in Rimouski," she replied, a wistful note in her voice. "It means only that life is good for nothing. A little hope, a little hate—and then, good night. Very sad, *n'est-ce pas*?"

Before the motel owner could answer, however, his telephone rang and he picked it up.

Nathalie sighed, and resumed sweeping the wall-to-wall electric-blue broadloom. (214)

With the high formality of these two mirrored scenes—the repetitions of "funny wavy hair" and Alfred de Musset's concise rhymed equation; the "electric-blue rug" expanding to the "wall-to-wall electric-blue broadloom"; "It is all so sad and cruel" condensing to "Very sad, *n'est-ce pas*?"; and "the whole tragic *histoire*" that constitutes the narrative within the frame—Greenan seals shut his intricately ordered *Can of Worms*.

CHAPTER EIGHT

"WHAT AN EDIFICE OF ARTIFICE!": *IT HAPPENED IN BOSTON?* (1968)

> "And he was a passionate, and wild and moody man, who became lost in reveries . . ."
>
> —"The Oval Portrait," Edgar Allan Poe

I.

> "The writer, for all his extravagances, did not sound crazy." (203)

There's a story behind the title that Greenan tells in his afterword to Modern Library's 20th Century Rediscovery edition of *It Happened in Boston?* (1968). "When I submitted the manuscript I called it *Alfred Omega*. My editor, Lee Wright . . . felt the word 'Boston' should be part of the title and suggested borrowing the sentence 'Who would believe such things could happen in Boston?' from the text. But Bennett Cerf considered that too long, so we settled on *It Happened in Boston?*" And now Greenan proceeds to whittle the title of his first novel down even further. His brother, a compositor, suggested it should be shortened to *In Boston?* while correspondents refer to it as *Boston?* and Greenan finally offers that the title might "be reduced to just the question mark, so that one might e-mail a friend and ask, 'Have you ever read ??'" (282), a reduction as spare as one by Beckett and sufficient to embody the interpretive, dialectical nature of the experience of reading a novel of an artist's quest for God, not obsequiously to greet Him but to dethrone and kill Him, and where the narrator's sanity and reality itself are in question.

He is mad, isn't he? The psychopath, according to William James, possesses a "love of metaphysics and mysticism which carry one's interests beyond the surface of the sensible world" (quoted in Kazin 165). What other explanation can there be for the novel's opening?

> Lately I have come to feel that the pigeons are spying on me. What other explanation can there be?
>
> The Public Garden across the way attracts them, which is natural enough since there are trees there and grass and water in the lagoon and, of course, a few fools who insist on scattering birdseed about. But it is hardly natural for them to flock to my window ledge early each morning and to remain there all day long. And it is certainly unnatural for them to peer into the room and scrutinize my newspaper clippings, my books and my private actions.
>
> Yesterday, as I sat in the Garden, I examined this apartment house. There are forty-six windows facing Beacon Street but only one—mine—was graced with those evil-looking birds. Forty-five without, one with. Significant.
>
> To be sure, I chase them, but they soon return. What draws them there? Why my window?
>
> This morning I put some poisoned bread outside the dining-room window. If nothing else, it should lure them away from my ledge, and if the stuff exhibits its custom-

> ary efficacy, some will perish. I can't hope to destroy every pigeon in the city, of course, but if I am lucky enough to get some of the ringleaders, it might serve to discourage the rank and file. (7)

The narrator's struggle with the Deity is no more one of belief than it was for Ahab; neither maddened character questions His existence or tyrannous implacability. The narrator's quest is, simply, to kill the Deity in order to revise a few things, such as the "total unintelligibility" of street addresses in phone books. "That will be revised, too" (12). To doubt the Deity doesn't enter the narrator's mind, but doubt is the dominant condition of the reader of *It Happened in Boston?* and the interrogative at the title's end is what dominates the diegesis. Are pigeons really spying on him, as he believes? Are his reveries real? "For the past year or so I have been developing a curious faculty—a kind of mind translation. This strange gift, which I suspect I share with few if any others in this world, permits me to visit different places in space and time and there assume an appropriate alien identity" (8). Are objects, such as pencils that keep breaking on him as he writes this book, "guided by a malevolent intelligence" (57), as he believes? Is this a novel of realism or eschatological fantasy? Is he mad or sane? Are we dealing in ultimate things or ravings? The novel's alpha word, "Lately"—time begins and it's already the past; its last word, "head"—the omega point, the final boundary. Is this the way out or in, the descent into the maelstrom or the return?

The last of the names employed by the narrator of *It Happened in Boston?* with the people he meets in Boston's Public Garden (principally: April Dandelion, who believes the narrator is a member of the Homicide Club; a small boy Randolph and his hand-puppet frog Sebastian; Mr. Beels, a crippled insurance salesman, and his factotum Johann) is Mr. Totality. The first is Alfred Omega.[24] Asked by Randolph what his first name is, Mr. Totality tells the boy that he used to have one, "but it wore out. People were always using it, you see. They all wanted to be friendly, I guess. Had it repaired once or twice, but in the end it just fell to pieces. Happened one day when my wife was calling me in . . . She never got past the first syllable and even that just crumbled into dust" (271). That's the problem with language and names and identities, especially if your sights are on a meeting with God—they disintegrate before your eyes and on your tongue, until all that's left is "the most enchanting oblivion" (in Robert Walser's typically peculiar phrase [120]). Though the plot of this novel is as tightly wound as any of the seven that would follow and the verisimilitudinous details as solid as a Boston park bench, *It Happened in Boston?*, the reading experience of it, often takes the reader to the edge of a *mise en abîme* such as the crumbling syllable story, and suddenly, when we gaze up again, we are within the abyss looking out at the world looking in.

Yet all we're reading is a tale narrated by a talented realistic painter (he grinds his own paints from only natural materials) who is duped into forging a da Vinci and falling for and marrying a woman named Veronica, whom he first speaks to in Lord's Gallery where she works, and who will leave him for the man behind the forgery, his devious dealer, Victor Darius. These and other events, patterns, foretellings, lead the narrator, whose name is as unknowable as YHWH's is unpronounceable, to seek out God for the purpose of killing Him for His multitude of crimes. With his wife gone, his two best friends dead, Benjamin Littleboy of suicide, Leo Faber of strychnine placed in a café's sugar bowl by

24 The narrator mentions his mother only in passing ("My mother died when I was seventeen" [17]); no mention is made of his earthly father.

the narrator himself, and six others also poisoned before Faber, Mr. Totality is ready in the end to meet God.[25]

The madman never knows he's mad, of course, though he's sane enough to have doubts if not about God at least about himself. "Ah well, maybe I am hopelessly mad" (59). "Minds have been known to crumble beneath lesser burdens than that which oppressed mine. Was all my thinking merely the symptom of some raging cerebritus? Was my search for God inspired by nothing more noble than a malfunctioning blood vessel in my brain or a blob of broken-down tissue in one of its convolutions?" (187). It helps that there are other characters as mad or madder than he to serve as contrast, a "crackbrain" musician he sees one day in the Garden, for example, making "a disagreeable series of squeaks and rattles . . . A pitiful spectacle. The authorities should do something about this plague of madness" (205). Yes, I may be insane, but the world itself is more crack-brained than I by far, as evidenced by the likes of Mr. Beels, an insurance salesman who "is either a maniac or some sort of confidence man" (169) or the Devil, and gaunt pigeon-loving April Dandelion with her Homicide Club notion. But if her paranoia matches the narrator's, she's still right to think that the narrator is part of the Homicide Club, even if the organization is only a conspiracy fantasy of hers. And it's April's

25 "Religion," William James wrote in his conclusion to *The Varieties of Religious Experience*, "is a monumental chapter in the history of human egotism . . . Religious thought is carried on in terms of personality, this being, in the world of religion, the one fundamental fact. Today, quite as much as at any previous age, the religious individual tells you that the divine meets him on the basis of his personal concerns" (412). When asked whether he thought the novel "antireligious," Greenan said, "No, the book is not antireligious. The narrator questions divine justice, but so does Job. So does Jesus . . . So do Dostoevsky, and Joyce, and I. B. Singer. Thinking men and women have challenged God on these matters for thousands of years. The subject of divine justice is a major problem for theologians. Indeed an argument could be made that all religions had their own origins in these inquiries" ("A Conversation with Russell H. Greenan").

sane madness that sends a Boston Irish cop into the narrator's room (she believes rightly that he's poisoning pigeons), where he finds the poison and realizes he's in the apartment of the Boston Borgia.

How quickly and darkly operates Greenan's *sinister dexterity.* When, in chapter 75 (of 93), the "I" discovers that Veronica and Victor have stolen everything from his studio and shipped it to Europe, he tells Leo in the next chapter, "They didn't leave a scrap. What would she want with work books and plaster fragments? I tell you, there's something extremely sinister about it all. They're an evil pair, Leo" (224). Even the simplest statements are riddled with ironies. "Go home and try to relax," Leo suggests, not knowing what that would entail for his distraught friend. "You're as coiled as a bedspring" (225), not knowing the narrator often lies beneath his bed staring at the bed coils, while all around him—in the air, in this world and others, in objects, and in some select characters like his wife, his art dealer, and his Deity—conspiracies swirl. Tired of telling jokes based on puns, those broken-backed word games that will appear throughout Greenan's subsequent work, the narrator asks Randolph if he "know[s] any serious questions." "Sure," Randolph replies. "Well, ask one for a change." And Randolph says, "How did God make Himself?" (188). "Is there more to the child than meets the eye?" wonders the narrator and reader. "His precocity is almost weird" (189).

II.

> "What if it is all groundless nonsense? What if I have only imagined these things? Casimir, the Bourg Angel and all the rest may be nothings—mere fancy." (278)

Midway through this book which begins *in medias res*, the narration still hasn't caught up to the present, as Greenan moves through his character's past lighting our way into his madness and justification for wanting to unseat God. He sows his plot with partial revelations about, variously: his narrator's marriage; the art careers of his and his two friends, the successful Leo Faber and the unsuccessful genius Benjamin Littleboy; Darius's duplicity, e.g. the scheme to trick the narrator into unwittingly forging a da Vinci. (Greenan's novel has the distinction of plotting to perfection the way to paranoia.) And, yes, the murders he's committing in order to take a meeting, so to speak, with God, whom he, with some justification, calls "this clumsy Architect of the universe . . . this insensate Scatterer of misery . . . this feelingless Father, this demon Deity" (145).

At best, God's absence is the problem; at worst, His malevolency. "Man was the dupe of God" (177)—God, the great con man, the Barnum of the Skies, the painter of masks, father of Ahab and the Whale and a river-boat confidence man and his masquerade, or "Prince of Condom," as Mary Urquhart in Greenan's *Heart of Gold* calls her first lover. Everywhere we see God's trickster hand at work, especially on the private world of the narrator. The objects that seem alive or possessed (manipulated) by spirits (doors, pencils, birds) are not signs of animism but examples of the extent of a possibly malevolent Deity's reach into his surrounds. Thus, the narrator has no reason to be forgiving. If this ex-artist, murderous madman were God, could creation not be improved? Isn't he not more worthy of Godhood than God Himself?

The real problem is, in two words, time and death, whether the issue is with the murder of the woman he witnesses as a child, or, while visiting a hospital with his art teacher Angelo Loupa, the girl whose dress caught fire from a birthday candle, or the suicide of Benjamin Littleboy, or the victims he has poisoned with the *nux vomica* he found in an antique apothecary chest he bought. How to remake time, how to overcome death: that's what the narrator must solve to escape the horror, overcome the conspiracies swirling around him. Death is what dominates. "Benjamin was dead, completely and utterly so and for eternity. Heaven, hell and the immortality of the soul meant nothing to me, and having rejected these theological conceits, I was left with only death—real death, total death, forever" (177). Death and death and death. "There are some outrages that cannot be permitted, some torments not to be borne" (145). No wonder that one of the novel's theological chapters (41) is followed by our first view of Littleboy's masterpiece "The Birth of Death," soon to be burned by Alfonzo de Reya, a paragon of Boston art society.

> The main figure, Death, had just hatched from a shiny blue-black egg in the center of the picture. He was not a large figure—scarcely half the size of the humans around him—but he dominated everything . . .
>
> The more I looked, the more convincing it all became. [Littleboy] had shown a prowess that he'd never revealed before. The picture was almost impossible. Everywhere I looked my eyes met vignettes of fear and fury. Men hacked limbs from women; dogs tore at the throats of screaming children; a piebald stallion stomped a bloody old man; a boy battered a gray kitten; a teenaged girl cut the throat of an infant; a gryphon, its beak speckled with grume, fed on a struggling redheaded man; a monstrous

> snake, its scales reflecting the light like shards of glass, crushed a bawling calf in its coils . . .
>
> "What's the source of that light?" I asked.
>
> "Ha! It's God," Benjamin said. "He's returning to heaven after hatching the egg. You'll notice He leaves his offspring behind." (147–49)

When the narrator tries to interest his dealer, Victor Darius, in Littleboy's work, Darius says, "Modern man wants no part of horror. He has lost the religious and philosophical beliefs necessary to cope with it" (155).

Littleboy leaves behind a son and a wonderful wife, Danielle. After "The Birth of Death," his artistic legacy, is burned, all that's left of it is one of his beloved rats. "Yes," he tells the narrator, "a black one in the extreme left-hand corner. He was meant to be looking out at the scene from the edge of the frame. He was the only sane figure in the thing" (163).[26] The painting was a masterpiece, but at

26 In Philip K. Dick's final novel, *The Transmigration of Timothy Archer* (1982), the narrator Angel Archer learns of the suicide of her father-in-law Bishop Archer's mistress, an amphetamine addict with a schizophrenic son. Angel drives to San Francisco in her Honda to meet with Bishop Archer, a man obsessed with the nature of God and finding the historical sources of Christ. Outraged by her father-in-law's indifference to his mistress's death, Angel writes, "There is a line somewhere in *Wozzeck* that translates out to, roughly, 'The world is awful.' Yes, I said to myself as I shot across the Bay Bridge not giving a fuck how fast I drove, that sums it up. That is high art: 'The world is awful.' That says it all. This is what we pay composers and painters and the great writers to do: tell us this; from figuring this out, they earn a living. What masterful, incisive insight. What penetrating intelligence. A rat in a drain ditch could tell you the same thing, were it able to talk. If rats could talk, I'd do anything they said" (180). Littleboy, who loved and protected rats, might well have appreciated this sentiment. These two theological fictions, though different in approach (Greenan's carnivalesque Gothic realism versus Dick's strict realism, at least in this novel), explore the madness inherent in theology.

what price? "'You are approaching the divine,' I said. 'Where it differs from nature, nature is at fault'" (150). The divine, it seems, always partakes of madness. Danielle, with her "gypsy blood," knows the painting "can bring only bad luck." And the narrator "could feel its madness" (150). After "The Birth of Death," Littleboy stops painting, wanders the street looking for fallen money, and plans a new painting, "Cosmogony," which "will reveal everything" (153). But this painting, which he says will produce "celestial melodies," he can't finish.

The narrator accuses God of "destroying beauty" because time destroys all art. But he is not cognizant, as was Nabokov, that art is a combination of beauty and pity, "for the simple reason that beauty must die: beauty always dies, the manner dies with the matter, the world dies with the individual" (Nabokov, *Lectures on Literature*, 251). Instead, he can only see God's injustice and vow to kill to Him. "Real explanations—that is what I would have. No longer could I tolerate the abasement and nullification of man" (177).

One day he wanders into "a poorly lit antique shop on Charles Street," where in a dark corner a "small, shiny brown face peered between an ancient coal scuttle and a dented tea chest and watched me even as I watched it." This is the Bourg Angel, "carved in high relief on the sliding door of an apothecary chest . . . with an expression that was vital and yet divinely detached." Convinced "that the little face, whatever its composition, contemplated me when I first discovered it" (53), he purchases the chest and puts the door on his mantel and begins to believe it is "a representation . . . of a being from another part of the universe—an ultra-human" (54). "That Monsieur Bourg is not mentioned in the art books of the world is incredible" (55), but so is the fate that awaits the art of Littleboy and the narrator. When he summons an angel using a formula he finds in a book (dead finch at the foot of the bed, a drawing of two triangles under his pillow) the Bourg Angel comes "like smoke from a chimney . . . out of her panel" (207). At first she acts imperious but soon is reduced by the narrator's Promethean demands to a terrified sprite. Perhaps God, too, may not be as powerful as he's been led to believe. If an angel fears the narrator, why wouldn't the Supreme Being?

The reader should wonder what kind of God the narrator would be, taking into account the trial by fire, fear, and betrayal he has endured and the murders he's committed. A sane God? In "Hawthorne and His Mosses," Melville wrote of the "sane madness of vital truth" found in Shakespeare (*The Piazza Tales* 244). Saturated in madness, deceit, and murder, Greenan's novels suggest that sanity and truth may have little in common. The *insane* madness of vital truth is the truth of God as the narrator sees it in Littleboy's masterpiece, "The Birth of Death." Birth and Death. The fusion we find in Beckett's *Waiting for Godot* when Vladimir says "Astride of a grave and a difficult birth. Down in the hole, lingeringly, the grave-digger puts on the forceps" (58), and in Melville's pun "grave-dug berth" (137) that Ahab descends to on the Pequod, and Ossie Peña's pitiful death in a laundromat dryer ("The shape of the drum forced him into a fetal position" [141]) in *A Can of Worms*. Such metaphysical horror that fuses life with death whelms the narrator of *It Happened in Boston?* so that, like Ahab, now madness maddened, he must kill the creator and perpetrator of death. When Randolph, the narrator's partner in jokes and puns, loses his hand-puppet frog Sebastian (Randolph suspects Mr. Beels took it), the narrator thinks, "What is the sense of separating Sebastian from Randolph or a mauve balloon from some other child? I hoped all that could be changed" (230). In the chapter preceding "The Grand Inquisitor" chapter of *The Brothers Karamazov*, Ivan tell his brother Alyosha to speak

> straight out, I call on you—answer me: imagine that you yourself are building the edifice of human destiny with the object of making people happy in the finale, of giving them peace and rest at last, but for that you must inevitably and unavoidably torture just one tiny creature, that same child who was beating her chest with her little fist, and raise your edifice on the foundation of her unrequited tears—would you agree to be the architect on such conditions? (245)

For both Ivan Karamazov and Alfred Omega, the horror of injustice and loss, specifically the loss of life, is too great to forgive God His non-intervention on this point.[27]

From a book he finds in a box of occult works a used book dealer fobs off on him, *The Life and Precepts of Jozef Casimir, The Wizard of Podolia, as Written by Himself*, translated from the Polish probably in the seventeenth century, the narrator learns how to summon angels and God. "The [formula] for summoning God requires the murder of 'seven innocents, without regard to sex or age so long as they be completely human,' after which you draw a spiral, mutter a few words and the Supreme Being makes His

27 Not for Alfred Omega such theosophical spins of the birth/death coin as Nabokov's Fyodor Godunov-Cherdyntsev's in *The Gift* (1963): "It is painful to leave life's womb. The deathly horror of birth" (311).

appearance. Nothing to it, once you're past the slaughter" (202). After reading Casimir's account of meeting God in an inn (a large yellow cat sits on God's shoulder), he observes: "The writer, for all his extravagances, did not sound crazy" (203).

Often the narrator, for all his extravagances, doesn't seem crazy either. In fact, his life seems in large part a preparation to become God. As a youth he studies with one Angelo (aka Seraphino) Loupa, "a vagabond Verrocchio, a misplaced Michelangelo, a Cellini born into a churlish era." One night, as a youth himself traveling in Greece, Loupa "saw Zeus standing in the street watching him" (34). Zeus, Loupa tells his pupil, "raised his hand and put a sign on me. I wanted to call to him but my heart was not even beating and I could not move my tongue in my mouth. When next I came to my senses, he was gone" (35). Loupa instructs his pupil in how to grind his own paints ("If you want real color, use real colors" [29]). Like Ignacio Never in *The Queen of America* who wishes to film human life as it is lived, the narrator is a realist who can "sketch and paint everything in sight, from the stately churches in Copley Square to the slavering chimpanzees in Franklin Park" (33).

By passing off the narrator's paintings as the work of old masters, Darius affirms the narrator's God-like qualities. The narrator can pass as various old masters, just as in his reveries he can become anyone. Like God, it is the artist who is "most conscious of eternity . . . Only he attempts to challenge God by creating that which has never existed before and may, if his work perishes, never exist again. Only he and God can produce beauty. Only he and God can make a world. Only he can compete with the Deity in matters of intellect and sensibility" (176). Once the fine points of theology are dismissed, we are "left with only death—real death, total death, forever." This the narrator will not forgive God, even if it means killing seven people to tell Him so.

> God knew perfectly well the results of His actions. He ordained the whole miserable system, and my modest prayers would never cause Him to alter it. I began to wonder if He thought beauty His own special preserve and that for this reason He would tolerate no encroachment by man. If that were so, what iniquity it was! My mind turned to other injustices. I brooded. I began to think of God as evil, as an ominous Dominus whose role was to enslave, torment, and ultimately destroy humanity. Man was the dupe of God. One afternoon this thought penetrated my mind to such a depth that I fell to beating myself on the face and head. My rage was like a holocaust. "Vengeance!" I screamed to my empty studio. (177)

If this sounds more like the naïve ravings of a youth or the rantings of an old Mark Twain, one must remember the events that have led the narrator to his position, among them the plot to erase his identity as an artist and the destruction of Littleboy's masterpiece "The Birth of Death" and Litttleboy's subsequent suicide, which, as it turns out, wasn't a suicide after all, but one of God's accidents. Littleboy has tried to hang himself, but changes his mind. "The noise that attracted his wife was the sound of his fingernails seeking purchase on the wall, which came into reach at the end of each swing of his body. We could see these pathetic scratches in the dirty plaster" (172). Danielle tries to help her poor rat-like husband find a hold, but "each time he freed a hand to loosen [the noose], his body would drop to the end of the rope. Try as she might, she couldn't hold him up alone. Each of these falls was accompanied by a sickening thud as the hemp tore into the flesh, muscle and bone of the neck" (172–73). After Littleboy's death, as the narrator says in a one-sentence chapter, "Not much went right after that" (174).

III.

> "He has woven a web of such intricacy that I cannot see the beginning or even imagine the end, but I am truly snared in its glittering filaments." (232)

i.

The burden of the plot of *It Happened in Boston?*, carried with formal grace by Greenan, is to make plausible the following recap the narrator delivers toward the novel's end as he contemplates jumping off the Cottage Farm Bridge:

> Who ever had greater cause to take his own life? Consider what I have had to endure . . . A faithless, empty-headed, burglarious woman for a wife and a conscienceless, philandering English phlebotomist for a business agent. This precious pair of vipers began it all. These two adders divided my life, subtracted my happiness and multiplied my misfortunes. It was they who tipped me into that maelstrom of false marcheses, mercenary Bergamese whores, slippery Italian counts, witless German art experts, vil-

> lainous Peruvian generals, paranoiac harpies, spiteful Russian cats, specious Polish wizards, spying pigeons, nosy janitors and ambitious Irish cops. My closest friend was driven to hang himself by my closest enemy. Somehow, through cunning insinuation and obscure machination, I was inveigled into murdering six poor strangers and the kind and generous Leo Faber—in the name of humanity! I have been slandered, lied to, cuckolded, robbed and persecuted. My lovely reveries have been snatched from my head and replaced by nightmares. The fruit of my years of labor—enough beauty to stock a museum—has been carried off to a foreign land, while one of my masterpieces has been plagiarized by a man dead five hundred years. I've been thwarted by an angel, duped by God and stalked by the Devil. Who would believe such things could happen in Boston? (277)

One reason we believe it could happen in Boston is because on various levels a generative dialectic operates. Take for example the way we begin *in medias res* and then back- and forward-track along a plot line of revelations ("detonations," the narrator calls them [240]) leading to the summary above. On page 11 the Bourg Angel is first mentioned; on page 12 we learn that his "criminal activities have acquainted [him] with many cafeterias," and that after dinner he likes to "read a little of my Casimir book . . . or study my newspaper clippings," but in none of these instances do we learn anything more than the name of the thing without revealing its past or meaning. Page 20 reveals that he's a murderer ("He came shortly after I killed the twin"). Pages 52 to 55 relate his purchase of the Bourg Angel. On page 67 we learn that he poisoned "the girl on Boylston Street and all the others," without us yet knowing who the others are. "I had hoped to go in search of a restaurant with a sugar bowl but the heat precluded this mild ambition" (74). "I've been afraid to continue my sugar-bowl hunt, even afraid to go into restaurants" (140). "I have spent the entire day wandering in and out of restaurants in Dorchester . . . No success" (181). "Word soon got about that I was willing to pay hard cash for a conversation with God" (185). On 196 we finally learn the full name and more about the Casimir book, *The Life and Precepts of Jozef Casimir, The Wizard of Podolia, as Written by Himself*; on page 202 at last the formula "for summoning God [which] requires the murder of 'seven innocents, without regard to sex or age so long as they be completely human,' after which you draw a spiral, mutter a few words and the Supreme Being makes His appearance." And now the past closes in on the present, the revelations about the murders (he's been putting particles of *nux vomica*, from the apothecary chest with the Bourg Angel carved on it, into sugar bowls in Boston restaurants and cafés to meet his quota) come fast. The twins at last on page 214, one of whom will be dead by page 218, his first kill. Ten pages later the sixth victim is dead, and the past merges with the present. "That was more than a month ago." Only the seventh victim is left, the final detonation.[28] "One edition carried a picture labeled at the top: Latest Target of Killer, but only the crown of a man's head was visible because of the fold in the page. I lifted it and turned it back to have a look at him." His seventh victim is Leo Faber, his only remaining friend and hope to untangle the plot and catch

28 One might find it of interest to compare *IHiB?* to the Val Lewton-produced film *The Seventh Victim* (1943), a somber study of religion, madness, devil worship, and fate.

Darius. "My eyes filled with blackness, as though a sable pall had dropped before my face" (260).

These periodic revelations substantiate the fiction's reality without ever (the question mark again that rings off each fact and fantasy of the text) confirming it. With a handful of reveries to other times and lands mixed in—Venice in 1380 (9); Gades as a fruit seller (20); "on the banks of the Lena, helping to unload pine logs from a barge" (62); "Japan during the revolution of 1867" while soldiers kill his brother (73); as a Medieval thief chased to a church (94–98); as a prospector for diamonds in Tijekem (125); in ancient Lydia about to fight the Persians (169); at last his first reverie: on a ship near "a walled city on the tip of a headland" (185–86); "a trip to Lindos on the island of Rhodes in the fifteenth century" (205)—this movement from present-day Boston into reveries of different times and places, narrows vortically, until they come together, like the points on God's helix that he will draw in order to summon his enemy.

The diastole and systole of the novel is its constant movement between the realistic and fantastic levels, the social and the private. On the realistic/social level the Irish cop is right that the bottle he's found in the narrator's apartment is "*Nux vomica*, me boyo, and . . . not *Dominus vobiscum*" (269). On the private/fantastic level, pigeons spy on Alfred Omega, wooden angels come alive, the Devil sells life insurance, and *nux vomica* may turn out to be, at least for seven dead people, the priest's "God be with you" blessing in the Latin mass. Beels thinks of Death as having "eyes that captivate the whole of mankind. From the depths of one of these somber orbs flows the murky light of inscrutability, while from the other streams the hard gleam of inevitability" (99). Inscrutability and inevitability: the two poles (alpha/omega) that energize this novel as surely as they do *Moby-Dick*. Further down the chain of the novel's DNA, even the chiasmus in a Chinese joke Alfred Omega tells Randolph—"Hi, Lo." "Lo, Hi" (14)—participates in the novel's dialectical energies.

ii.

How it clusters, collapses, connects, as if the entire edifice sat precariously on each particle of text, turn of tale, from a simple pun (Alfred Omega) to a private joke—when the narrator at fourteen asks his private art tutor who has had to give up his unprosperous school "where I might find another instructor whose fees might be comparable to his own, he thought a while and then, laughing as if at a private joke, suggested a Mr. Loupa in the South End" (25). Loupa, with the name's echo of wolf, loopiness, madman. Pupil, meet your mirror and maker. Of course Mr. Loupa lives in a "battered tenement on Tremont Street" built in the Greenan Gothic style with "a plump gray rat [that] dropped from the rim of a half-covered garbage can" (25) as its gray usher, and the novel's first rat of many.[29] Benjamin Littleboy feeds, identifies with, and paints rats, and dies like one; April Dandelion feeds pigeons.

Pigeons and rats scrambling and fluttering all over a madman's Boston. And cats, too, of course, natural enemy of bird and rodent. "At the age of four," the realist tells us with justified immodesty, "I became obsessed with our cat, and there was a shoebox filled with drawings of this animal that would have done credit to many of the budding Rembrandts who strut each year from our schools of art" (18). For his first Grand Guignol performance of a death, Greenan, with Poe looking over his

29 The anagram of RAT should not go unnoted.

shoulder, chooses "a Russian Blue cat that Veronica had bought" named Mitya. Poe's Pluto in "The Black Cat" was also procured by the narrator's wife. Initially both narrators are fond of the domestic addition. Poe: "Pluto—this was the cat's name—was my favorite pet and playmate. I alone fed him, and he attended me wherever I went about the house" (321). Greenan: "In the beginning we were close friends, this cat and I; I never forgot his meals nor neglected to change the sand in his box; I patted him occasionally and allowed him to rub himself against my trouser leg as often as he desired" (85). But after being taken over by "the Fiend Intemperance," Poe's character changes and one day, possessed by the "fury of a demon," takes from his "waistcoat-pocket a pen-knife, opened it, grasped the poor beast by the throat, and deliberately cut one of its eyes from the socket!" (322). For Greenan's narrator, "Time and familiarity . . . soon impaired our friendship" (85).

> One day, when the animal seemed to be forever under foot, I flew into a rage and punched him in the face.
>
> The results of this blow were two in number. First, Mitya developed a profound hatred of me and would bite or scratch me at every opportunity and, second, one of his eyes became slightly displaced in his head so that he always seemed to be looking in two directions at once. (86)

—not unlike, these eyes, how Beels sees the implacable and inevitable eyes of Death.

The narrator of "The Black Cat" hangs Pluto, in full knowledge this is "a deadly sin that would so jeopardize my immortal soul as to place it—if such a thing were possible—even beyond the reach of the infinite mercy of the Most Merciful and Most Terrible God" (323). Eventually, after the cat's *Doppelgänger* shows up, he'll bury an axe in his wife's brain. (He thinks about "cutting the corpse into minute fragments, and destroying them by fire" [327]—Kevin Reedy's preferred method of disposing of his victims in *A Can of Worms*—but chooses entombment instead, Poe's preferred method and Algernon Pendelton's at the end of his story.)

Greenan's narrator is obsessed with the cat's eyes. "Whenever I raised my eyes, I could be sure that he would be there, searing me with a most deadly stare—one eye transfixing me by the shortest route, the other cleverly turning my flank and coming at me in a wide arc. There was no escape" (86). (The old man's eye was the trigger for the narrator's murder in "The Tell-Tale Heart.") Wobble-eyed Mitya will drink milk laced with *nux vomica*. "[A]s my recollection of Latin indicated . . . this meant vomit nut, I thought it would be a good joke to sprinkle a soupçon of the stuff on my foe's bowl of milk" (86).

> Ten minutes later I felt his eyes upon me, and turning, saw him crouching on the sideboard in the next room. The sight gave me a frightful shock, for not only was he treating me to his most potent, cockatrice glare, but he was grinning broadly as well. Alice's grinning cat on a printed page is undeniably amusing, but believe me, it's a different matter altogether when you come upon such a phenomenon in the flesh. The animal's smile seemed to expand even while I watched, until it split his face like a wound. His eyes, meanwhile, gradually closed in the process, emitting from their disoriented pupils an almost

> tangible ray of concentrated hatred. I sat spellbound, the hair rising on my nape. As the pink lips of the creature stretched ever wider, his small, sharp teeth, wet and glistening, came ever more into view, and I could see that they were tightly clenched. One of his ears twitched nervously and his whiskers vibrated from the tension of his facial fibers. Suddenly his head jerked back and he stood up. His tail became rigid as a length of a broomstick and his four long legs extended stiffly, making him appear abnormally tall. A moment later he toppled from the sideboard. (87).

Not that he's dead yet. Greenan still has three paroxysms in fifteen minutes—half a page—to go before finishing the cat off. Much later, Alfred Omega will read up on the effects of strychnine. "During that brief period the body is racked with spasms of agony, the face wears a frightful smile and the eyes an expression of the most awful terror. It did not seem like an easy method of ceasing to exist" (158). This "*rissus sardonicus*" (227) produced by ingesting strychnine spreads its grin across the novel's sky.

The next cat we encounter (it has a certain Lewis Carroll pedigree) is from the Casimir book, a large yellow cat sitting on God's shoulder in a Krakow inn.

> Where it came from I could not tell, but its appearance was less cause for wonder than its subsequent actions, for after leaping to the floor, it bounded across the room, ran up the far wall, raced upside-down across the ceiling and returned to my companion's shoulder by way of

> the wall behind him. There it rested only long enough to lick its whiskers before it vanished before my eyes. (199)

And the final cat is spectral. On the night before he summons God, the sleepless night when he keeps seeing in his mind's eye Faber's death ("the hideous grin and the twitching muscles" (262),

> well into night, I heard three chimes of a church bell and found myself sitting at the window, staring at the street lamps in the Garden. Two in particular, because of their seeming proximity, resembled giant orange eyes—and not just any eyes, but a familiar pair. One appeared slightly larger than the other. I suddenly realized that they were Mitya's crooked occuli and I leaped from my chair and ran from the window. (262–63)

iii.

"We wove a tale," Victor says. "Then we found a girl with a quattrocento face and brought her to America," not the daughter of a marquis, as Alfred Omega believed, but "a prostitute from Bergamo" (245). After he hears Darius's explanation of the "ultimate in deception," he thinks, "What an edifice of artifice! There had to be a chink in so complex a structure" (250). Perhaps, but not in the novel's plot (the sequence of events as arranged by the author) or its pattern of motifs or its dialectical loops, signified by the helix, God's sign, the narrator must draw. Greenan's spiral descends from Poe's maelstrom and Melville's vortex, the one in the end that swallows the crew of the Pequod, all except Ishmael, who escapes on his own birth-of-death lifebuoy coffin. The narrator of *It Happened in Boston?* has followed as devious a path as the Pequod, though his genius and madness make him as much an Ahab returned to tell the tale as an Ishmael.

What but form will take the artist to God, deliver him to Him? "If the gods reached the heavens through a form," writes Roberto Calasso in *Literature and the Gods*, "how much more will men have need of form if they are to reach the gods" (150–51). In his apartment Alfred Omega sits down and, as instructed by Casimir,

> drew a small circle in the center of the sheet and filled it in so completely that it looked like a hole in the paper. Beginning there and working outward, I traced a neat, perfectly proportional spiral. The room suddenly grew still. I worked deliberately and with a steady hand, and when after the fourth loop I ended the coil, I did so with a second black ball exactly the size of the first. Putting the pencil aside, I surveyed the design. The concentric lines formed a whirlpool that pulled the eye into the spot at the center, while the spot itself appeared to expand and gape. (265)

At this extreme level of formality, where spirals engender form, order takes on new energies, signs appear everywhere, often with their signifiers detached. As if, like Oedipa Maas "trapped at the centre of some intricate crystal" (Pynchon, *The Crying of Lot 49* 92), the reader, as the signs accumulate, becomes a participant in the novel's paranoia.[30] Before he asks for the last

30 After seeing "the WASTE symbol" on an old man's ring, Oedipa Maas in *The Crying of Lot 49* (1966) "looked around, spooked at the sunlight pouring

time the narrator's name, Randolph mentions that his cousin Claude, who has a hat just like the one the narrator is wearing ("To alter my appearance, I put on a gray straw hat and an olive linen jacket that I hadn't worn in years" [270]) is seven years old. Seven days to create the universe, thinks the reader, seven murders to meet God.[31]

Events in the novel are timed to a Kleistian, sharp-edged precision.[32] At the moment he's finished the rites to call forth the Deity—the seven names of his victims ("I inhaled and exhaled seven times"), the prayer to the "All of everything," the exact moment when the last word of the prayer ("Thee") leaves his lips, he touches the center of the spiral he's drawn. Something momentous, as in the work of all concentric-minded Romantics, must now ensue, in this case three to four seconds of motionless silence, followed by "a sharp and imperious knock upon the apartment door" (266). Not God, alas, but an Irish cop, who discovers, as the narrator hides under his bed, the bottle of *nux vomica* and the clippings he's saved about the murders.[33]

---

in all the windows, as if she had been trapped at the centre of some intricate crystal, and said, 'My God'" (92).

31 To continue the speculative or paranoid criticism we can note that G is the seventh letter of the alphabet and wonder if this is why there are 93 rather than 100 chapters in the narrator's tale.

32 The reference to Kleist is not random. The narrator of *IHiB?* reads, besides a book on potions and parts of a book on Tritheme, "some stories by von Kleist" (205), including, I'm assuming, Kleist's great revenge novella, "Michael Kolhaas," and "Earthquake in Chile," narrated *in medias res* with its characters *in extremis*, in the whirl of *Zufall* (the German coincidence/fate/chance).

33 Under his bed the narrator eavesdrops, that overworn technique of melodrama, but unlike its use in, say, Lermontov's *A Hero of Our Time*, this is its only appearance in *IHiB?* For a discussion of eavesdropping in Lermontov, see Nabokov's "Translator's Foreword" in the translation by him and his son. The difference, in part, between these nineteenth- and twentieth-century Romantics is in the relationship of plot to fate, technique to coincidence, with

From this point, the novel's narrative vise tightens as surely as at the end of *Nightmare* Axel Shadmeister's G.A.B.A. (Gravity Actuated Ball Automaton) ratchets into place, "lift[s] the telephone from its cradle" (205), and thus effectively ends the novel by ending the narrator's (earthly) life on the birth/death axis of its final word (*cradle*). But the question remains (always in *It Happened in Boston?* the question remains) on which level of the Alpha/Omega dialectical spiral is the narrator at story's end? Or does he simply land on . . . I mean, in his head, as the last word of the novel (*head*) suggests?

"I, who had always cherished order, was now as disarrayed as everything else in this discordant world" (276). The closer he gets to the ultimate formality of God, as exemplified in his helical drawing, the more disordered his world becomes. This, too, is part of the novel's dialectical dynamic. "My brain was a Gordian knot of doubt and perplexity" (278). After contemplating suicide, his thoughts turn again along their spiral: "Isn't it entirely possible that every move in this intricate chess match, from the subtle opening to the dreadful endgame, was designed solely to entice me into the trap of self-destruction?" (278).

IV.

> "I was convinced . . . that the reveries were in some way connected with my mission and that they would soon lead to other phenomena even more remarkable." (193)

Greenan less reliant on the latter and able to fuse plot to fate, so that no holes appear when his complex mantraps close.

In the house of fiction, theological narratives reside in a special room (upstairs, back) decorated in Gothic realism where metafiction may sleep with fantasy, because God, as Ludwig Feuerbach proposed in his *Das Wesen des Christentums* (1841), is always and only a concept, though regrettably turned by most humans into hard logic-defying fact.[34] From these premises theological fictions rise.[35] At this level of abstraction, one

---

34 "Consciousness of God is self-consciousness, knowledge of God is self-knowledge" (Feuerbach 192). The proper study of God, then, would be the study of human beings, and, by extension, the books they write.

35 William Harrison's Randle Fast in *The Theologian* (1965) believes "that after all my rash skepticism and calculated heresy I might, indeed, someday come face to face with a little white-bearded old gentleman with an angry fistful of lightning bolts and no sense of humor whatsoever who will be none other than Yahweh, Great Spirit, God Almighty Himself" (7). For Fast (and Alfred Omega), "Theology would push me toward darkened doors: into mysticism, dualism, the psychic dream worlds" (11), and for both characters murder will become a means to God. Madness and loneliness is also an issue in Harrison's "Weatherman: A Theological Narrative" (1973) from the collection *Rollerball Murder* (1974) and in Robert Coover's theological novel *The Universal Baseball Association, Inc., J. Henry Waugh, Prop.* (1968) which holds the same copyright year as *IHiB?* 1968 was also the year A. J. Langguth's *Jesus Christs* appeared—a good year, at least for God and His avatars as fictional characters. For the record, however, *IHiB?* did not appear until January 1969.

In fact the decade of the '60s saw a variety of novels with theological concerns. A partial list would include: *A Canticle for Leibowitz* by Walter Miller (1960), *The Violent Bear It Away* by Flannery O'Connor (1960), *Morte d'Urban* by J. F. Powers (1962), *The Centaur* by John Updike (1963), *Cat's Cradle* by Kurt Vonnegut (1963), *A Case of Conscience* by James Blish (1964), *The Wapshot Scandal* by John Cheever (1964), *The Three Stigmata of Palmer Eldritch* by Philip K. Dick (1964), *Do, Lord, Remember Me* by George Garrett (1965), *The Theologian* by William Harrison (1965), *At Play in the Fields of the Lord* by Peter Matthiessen (1965), *Giles Goat-boy* by John Barth (1966), *The Origin of the Brunists* by Robert Coover (1966), *Omensetter's Luck* by William H. Gass (1966), *The Fixer* by Bernard Malamud (1966), *A Smuggler's Bible* by Joseph McElroy (1966), *The Crying of Lot 49* by Thomas Pynchon (1966), *Rosemary's Baby* by Ira Levin (1967), *A Hall of Mirrors* by Robert Stone (1967), *The Confessions of Nat Turner* by William Styron (1967), *Lord of Light* by Roger Zelazny

that posits a participative Deity, fantasy often partakes of madness. Either it's me that's mad, Greenan's characters say, or it's the world. In *It Happened in Boston?* the narrator *knows* it's the world. After all, he is an inventor of worlds in his painting. "You have created a world, my good fellow, an entire world, really," says Darius (49). His reveries, too, are possibly inventions of other worlds. But one shouldn't forget that someone really does control this paranoiac's life, that "Mr. Totality" is a recipient/victim of a controlling hand, the one responsible, after all, for the events that lead this God-in-training to seek God in order to rectify His mistakes. And whom can we hold responsible for putting Alfred Omega through his terminal metaphysical paces? Russell H. Greenan, whose "clever Le Sur" (Rus[s]el[l] in reverse) is credited with the couplet "Guard grimly your veracity, /

(1967), *Black Easter* by James Blish (1968), *Dagon* by Fred Chappell (1968), *The Universal Baseball Association, Inc. J. Henry Waugh, Prop.* by Robert Coover (1968), *The Artificial Traveller* by Warren Fine (1968), *Jesus Christs* by A. J. Langguth (1968), *Couples* by John Updike (1968), *When the War Is Over* by Stephen Becker (1969), *Galactic Pot-Healer* by Philip K. Dick (1969), *Blind Man with a Pistol* by Chester Himes (1969), *Horn* by D. Keith Mano (1969), and carries over into the '70s with *A Maze of Death* by Philip K. Dick (1970), *Principato* by Tom McHale (1970), *The Day After Judgment* by James Blish (1971), *End Zone* by Don DeLillo (1972), *The Assassination of Spiro Agnew* (unpublished, 1972; excerpts at assassinationspiroagnew.blogspot.com) by Steven Janiszewski, and *Child of God* by Cormac McCarthy (1973), among many others.

Though all of these novels have theological concerns, I would categorize only about half of them as theological fictions, by which I have in mind a prose work of whatever length that has as its conceptual underpinning, consciously or not, a Feuerbachian understanding that God was created out of the mind of man. (This is not to say that the God-Mind, or God-out-of-mind, doesn't wield immense, though hardly omniscient powers over His flock.) Seen in these, so to speak, Feuerbachian terms, a theological fiction would be self-aware (though not necessarily overtly reflexive) of the fictive nature of all its characters, including any Deity or avatar of the Same. In the beginning indeed was the Word.

With desp'rate pertinacity" (10).[36] The control exhibited by the creator of *It Happened in Boston?* is carnivalesque, a top spinning in infinity, a perfected romanticism. Which is not to say that Alfred Omega belongs in a Queneau novel (e.g. *Zazie*; *The Flight of Icarus*), some of whose characters are aware of their fictive nature[37]; he's a "real" person caught in a theistic trap who must seek out and destroy the Deity. Character, meet your God. And kill him. This act is never shown, however. God, if this is God we see at the end (and not St. Peter or St. Augustine), yields.

> The old man stepped forward and I saw that he held a white velvet cushion upon which rested a truncated crystal, one of luminescent azure. With great dignity he set the cushion on the ground, lifted the crystal and advanced toward me.
>
> I saw then, that it was a crown. He placed it on my head. (283)

No surprise that this head trip of a novel ends with a crowned head or that crowns are woven through the text (and throughout Greenan's oeuvre). What exists that's not inside the head? asked Berkeley. (Not God, Feuerbach responds.) "Edward Young called

---

36 Other anagrammatic inscriptions by Greenan in later novels, as noted earlier, are Rengane, Enganar, and Sursell. "The text is a fetish object, and *this fetish desires me*," wrote Roland Barthes. "The text chooses me, by a whole disposition of invisible screens, selective baffles: vocabulary, references, readability, etc. and, lost in the midst of a text (not *behind* it, like a *deus ex machina*) there is always the other, the author" (27).

37 Though no Greenan character is as purely ludic or self-aware as Zazie's Uncle Gabriel in *Zazie dans le métro* (1959), there is a sense that Gabriel's reminder not to "forget the art in it though. It's not only fun, it's art" (175) is ever present in Greenan's work.

death 'the crown of life' and I find that both accurate and beautiful" (98–99). Littleboy's painting "The Tower of Babel" features General Jorge de Reyna as a donkey (Reyna will purchase and consign to flames Littleboy's masterpiece "The Birth of Death"), whose "crown hung from one long ear" (128). Even April Dandelion, no matter the season, wears "a high-crowned, broad-brimmed hat, the color of tarnished brass" (60). And in the newspaper that will identify his seventh victim, Mr. Totality at first sees "only the crown of a man's head . . . visible because of the fold in the page" (260).

While he spirals upward to the crown that awaits him at the end, back in Boston he spirals down. "Should I flee? Should I surrender? Should I live or die? Was I right or wrong? Wise or stupid? Mad or sane? I leaned against the stoplight stanchion and my eyes filled with tears. I wanted to shrink—to grow smaller, to shrivel and contract until I was no more than a mote and then, absolutely nothing at all" (278–79). When he escapes from his apartment, the signs he can't help but read as portents (no more than he could the congregation of pigeons on his window ledge) begin to proliferate triadically, as if born from the novel's dialectical energies; we are nearing the threshold, the crossroads, the trivium and an escape into a crystalline, geometric city. He encounters in the Garden 1) Randolph, 2) Beels, 3) April Dandelion. Randolph offers him a piece of Turkish taffy and finds out the narrator is calling himself "Mr. Totality." To Beels he says he has killed God and has Him in the shopping bag, which makes Beels from his wheelchair shout "Seize him, Johann . . . Seize the ruffian."

> Who is that man? I wondered. What's his game? Is he a detective? Some kind of an agent provocateur? I ran lightly but swiftly. Then a new and far more curious

> thought came to me. Those streaks of gray in his hair—were they really that or something else? I got only a fleeting view of them. Might they not have been—horns? Yes, horns! Was the fellow Old Nick himself? And those tiny, tiny shoes—did they hide hooves? Yes, yes. It could be. It could be and it would explain a great deal. His talk of contracts and of it being too late. He was after a hellish compact. Wait! Before he fell, did he shout, "Get him—fast," or was he saying in his outlandish accent, "Get him—Faust"? What about that? Was the silent Johann the ambitious Dr. Faust? Is it possible? Could it really be? The world is coming apart. This rickety universe has at last begun to crumble (274)

—crumble, that is, as it tilts to allegory.[38] Then April Dandelion "grasped my wrist," and accurately names him: "Poisoner... Killer! Murderer!" and runs beside him, "her gaunt face contorted by fury and her yellow hat flopping about precariously on her head," since she is a mad but bright spring weed. After "the ground beneath me was rocked by an ear-shattering clap of thunder" (274), he raises his fist and "bellow[s] defiantly, 'You missed me, You great, silly Ass!'"—reducing the Deity to the level of Alfonso de Reya, the destroyer of Littleboy's masterpiece.

38 Though not to the allegorical extent one finds in Willliam Gaddis's *The Recognitions* (1955), where the Mephistophelian character is named Recktall Brown. Gaddis's baroque, maximalist masterwork, like Greenan's *It Happened in Boston?,* is saturated with God talk and mystical signs. In addition, these novels' respective protagonists, Wyatt Gwyon and Alfred Omega, paint forgeries, but Wyatt does so knowingly. Both are also murderers (Wyatt's one to Omega's seven), and both are on a religious quest. But Greenan's narrator is not looking for redemption and Wyatt isn't out to kill God, and *Boston?* isn't a symphonic satire of modernity and automation but a masterwork of another kind.

Catching "a glimpse of myself in a store window," the narrator sees "a picture of desolation. I, who had always cherished order, was now as disarrayed as everything else in this discordant world" (276). Then, after contemplating suicide, and recapitulating his life, he's given three signs. 1) Attached to the back fender of a motorcycle, a sign reads "*Give us a smile, ya slob!*";[39] 2) he finds Randolph's Turkish taffy "[s]tuck to the sock" he uses to wipe the rain off his face, and 3) he picks up the "banknotes, gripped in the jaws of an outsized clothespin" that Benjamin had described in a dream. "Your recurring dream, the orange hat, the clothespin—I remember it all. Thank you, thank you, Benjamin, my old friend" (280).

> A broad beam of sunlight fell through a hole in the black clouds and landed at my feet. I eyed it suspiciously. Another sign? It looked like a spotlight. Is He trying to make friends with me? Does He seek a reconciliation, an end to the war? He must be frightened. I must have put a scare in Him. And You have good reason to be afraid, God! Oh yes. I will find You one day, and when I do, I'll straighten out Your spiral for You and tie a knot in it as well. Yes, even if it is as vast as the one in Andromeda—with my bare hands. Then it will no longer be You and me, God, but Me and you. I will have it all. I will capture infinity for eternity.
>
> And Benjamin—I will make you an archangel. And you one, too, Leo. Yes, that is what I will do. Why not? And all my victims—Janice and Aldo and the rest—you

39 Of course the signified of the "smile" is also the clenched smile from strychnine poisoning.

> will all be seraphim. I give you my word. That is how it will be. I will bring everyone who has ever lived back to life. Never again will anyone die. I will kill death! (281)

Is this beam of light truly one of the messages sent down by the Deity or only the narrator's delusional reading at a time of extreme, annihilation-confronting stress? Whatever, his interior monologue addressed to his White Whale and his victims is rudely and realistically interrupted by a "Hey, mac!" coming from a car out of which two men will chase him to a building with "three arched entrances set at the top of a flight of broad granite steps" (282), a building that perhaps has more than a coincidental relationship to an earlier reverie when, as a medieval burglar, he's chased by a mastiff to a church's "three familiar arched doorways with their blackened, nail-studded doors. I make for the center one, anxious to put its bulk between me and the monster at my heels" (97). But the center door will not open, just as it won't when he tries to open the center door in Boston. "What kind of church is this that locks its doors?" thinks the medieval thief. He has had to "cut the thongs and let my treasure slip from my shoulders," in order to "appease my pursuers" (97). In Boston, similarly, as if "acting on behalf of the universal malignancy" (Beckett, *Mercier and Camier* 26), "the silly shopping bag, weakened by the rain, burst. Out came the Bourg Angel, my underwear, all my papers, the bottle of strychnine and the roll of money" (282). After shouting "Damnation," he tries the center door three times, but it will not open. The signs have changed again; no longer are they favorable.

> It was too late to try the other doors and impossible to evade [the two men] if I fled back down the stairs. Suddenly I realized that it was over. Suddenly I knew that

> the end had come at last. Suddenly I saw that I was in the final trap; that I was, once and for all, terminated. The men came unhurriedly. I looked out over their heads at the speeding traffic. Raising my arms, hands in fists, I screamed. (282)

The three revelations behind the three *Suddenly*'s signal his termination and his triumph, his end and his new beginning. Here, at the moment of annihilation, he crosses over. How? Having reached his *terminus ad quem*, where else can he go but through the rent in reality's fabric, produced at the boundary of things, where *term* and *through* reveal their shared etymology in the Sanskrit *tarati*,—and what lies on the other side is the perfect city, the City of God.

> At the end of the road was a city on a hill, surrounded by a topaz wall of striking symmetry. Parallelepiped houses of colored crystal rose imperiously above this marvelous parapet. A great dipyramid balanced in perfect equilibrium upon its apex. An egg-shaped structure lay on its side on an oval platform near a ring, seven or eight stories high and made of octagonal bricks. Two flawless spheres of equal size sat one above the other. A massive honeycomb edifice, its cells utterly precise, appeared to float above the ground like a kite. There was a dodecahedron resting easily on the knife-edged juncture of two of its planes and a lovely scroll-like building whose curves were a joy to see. (282–83)[40]

40 "And before the throne *there was* a sea of glass like unto crystal: and in the midst of the throne, and round about the throne, *were* four beasts full of eyes before and behind." Revelation 4:6 (King James Version)

The Lord Mayor of St. Augustine's City of God is about to retire in favor of our narrator, who with his painterly eye notes first the forms about him: parallelepipeds, a dipyramid (twice three, like the two triangles he put under his pillow to summon an angel), an "egg-shaped structure . . . on an oval platform near a ring" (echoing the hard-boiled eggs that are the narrator's main nutriment), "seven or eight stories high and made of octagonal bricks" (seven or eight, because seven is the terminal number of names, and we need an eighth to start over again). And then the numbers multiply into "A massive honeycomb edifice" (what an edifice of artifice) that "appeared to float above the ground." And finally we move on to the archetypal twelve sides of the dodecahedron, and Greenan's terrible building for the first and last time is transformed into a "scroll-like building whose curves were a joy to see."

Beyond the forms, more amazing for the ex-painter are the colors—garnet, amethyst, "transparent terra-cotta and steel-blues." With the exception, perhaps, of that terra-cotta, the perfect city is all jewels and metals, reflective, geometrical. And above the city the sky is a "bronze bowl encrusted with a pair of blood-red suns whose rich beams flashed through the countless prisms of the houses and reflected from the millions and millions of minute surfaces" (283). (Are those "blood-red suns" that flash their "rich beams" the eyes of God or Mitya's eyes or Death's come back to haunt the narrator even in his fantasy?) Everything that meets the eye has been constructed with the care the narrator himself lavished on what he painted or sculpted. But of the two worlds, the one the narrator attempted to recreate with exact mimicry is the more richly detailed and complex. Heaven, if this is Heaven and not a dream vision out of a madman's final reverie, is idealized perfection, harmony, peace. "And how delightfully proportioned it all was. Each form—incredibly exact, intrinsically—harmonized completely with the whole. Each shade of color blended beautifully with all the others. Nowhere were there clashes, rough edges or cacophony. The city was perfect" (283).

The "twenty or twenty-five berobed people" who walk toward him "in sedate procession" with the one who will crown him being "an elderly man with a wispy beard at the head," have faces "like flowers"—and the flower-like hand of Randolph opens again in the reader's memory as Randolph offers the narrator for the first time some candy. "'Want a jujube?' His small hand emerged from the depths of his shirt pocket and opened like a somewhat grimy flower to reveal a small gummy object covered with fuzz" (13). The narrator refuses the offering and then is asked what his name is and the narrator replies "Alfred Omega." And now at the moment only minutes from when he crosses over, he accepts the offering, must have, for two pages before he enters the perfect city he wipes his face with a sock he's pulled out of his shopping bag filled with all that remains of his possession and finds stuck to the sock a "triangular-shaped piece of white candy." Yes, the sacrament is triform, and of foreign origin. " 'Turkish taffy,' I murmured, putting it in my mouth. 'What a good boy you are, Randolph' " (280). When Randolph offered it to him this (first to last) final time ("Want some Turkish taffy? It's good. Don't you like candy?" [271]), he accepted it, though we never see him doing so. Instead Randolph again asks him his name ("Mr. Totality" is the response) and poses once more a question regarding the naming and attributes of things. "If lemons are sour all the time, how can they tell when they're ripe?" Randolph asks, and in reply to the narrator's answer that unripe lemons are green, asks, "How can they tell with limes?" (271). Indeed there may be more "to the child than meets the eye" (189).

But what in God's name does the ending mean? No, that's not the question. Rather: What's it going to be? Sane or mad? Heaven or Hell, or Nothing-at-All, or only back into the body of the book and the head from which it all came? It's a wish-fulfillment dream. He's mad. He's dead but crowned God in the afterlife and has made no changes on earth because 1) it's impossible or 2) irrelevant or 3) what we readers and earthlings deserved all along. It's a confession from beyond the grave. He's made a total translation. It's only a reverie and the cops are going to bring him in. Foucault (on Roussel) speaks of the "anguish before too many and too few signs" (165), a description that suits our narrator's feelings and the reader's of *It Happened in Boston?* To accept any sign as definitive entails belief, and belief madness, especially in a world as deceitful as the narrator's, where the possibility really does exist that pigeons are God's spies.[41] On the other hand, doubt, too, can lead the metaphysician down the road of madness through an excess of polysemy which this novel may be accused of possessing, as if its author had ingested Hawthorne's "formula of alternative possibilities" (Winters 170).

As in spiritual comedies such as Nabokov's *Ada* and Quinn's and my *A Newcomer's Guide to the Afterlife*, *It Happened in Boston?* offers yet another further possibility—that it has passed from the other world back into this one. A crown is placed on his head and somehow the *unnamable* has sent this book back to us from the great whatever. Close to two hundred pages earlier, Beels has said, "Edward Young called death 'the crown of life' and I find that both accurate and beautiful" (98–99). If this makes as likely that the One-of-Many-Names winds up in Beels's hell (since Beels/Beelzebub is the one serving up this instance of the leitmotif) as much as in God's heaven, it equally suggests that, by relating his

41 Belief also allows him to murder seven people, two finches and a cat. No, the cat was an accident. No, an experiment he's willing to undertake because, like Poe's nameless narrator in "The Black Cat," he is possessed by the spirit of the Perverse and a hatred of his wife strong enough to transfer it to her cat. No, etc.

tale back to us (via Russell H. Greenan and Random House circa 1968–9), he has evaded "the irresistible personality, the grand persuader" Death. Through a rent in its narrative fabric, Alfred (Mr. Totality) Omega has passed between worlds.

Chapter 20, one of the novel's "theological" chapters (in its entirety below), foreshadows this possibility.

> When I was a boy, I wanted to see God. I believed that if I walked straight down Commonwealth Avenue, He would be there at the end. When I discovered that the world was round and that such a promenade would only bring me back to my starting point, I was chagrined, but only for a while. I determined to walk down Commonwealth Avenue but not to follow the contour of earth. I would walk straight, straight—on into the void, past the sun and the planets, past the stars and the nebulae and, without the smallest deviation, right to God. What Columbus did to my first scheme, Einstein did to my second. Still, I have not lost my desire to see Him. In those days, however, I had a great love for Him. Now I would like to ask Him some questions. (73)

Follow the dialectic. When I was a boy. Then I discovered. I determined. Then I discovered again. A to B equals C which forms a new A and its new B and new, greater C—still, nonetheless (the dialectic whirls on), the desire remains to make things right, to correct the self by correcting the maker of the self, God of all gods. Wouldn't you, if you were Alfred Omega/Perry G. Bolide/Mr. Barber/Myron Scopas/Giacomo Vermicelli/Lindsey Eiderdown/Mr. Totality? And if you are all these names and more, the Unnamable One, and if you've killed seven people in order to take a meeting with God, why not play the "Spinner of space and substance" in his own game, and yourself remake space, remodel substance, by performing the child's dream and walking "straight, straight—on into the void, past the sun and the planets, past the stars and the nebulae and, without the smallest deviation, right to God"?

This (possible) method of escape is also foreshadowed in a bit of dialogue by Darius. "I've always had an inclination toward intrigue and skullduggery," he tells the narrator. "A weakness, no doubt, but it was Leonardo, appropriately enough, who said, 'A straight line offers the most resistance'" (245). The straight line is the narrator's escape to another world, just as he had imagined it as a child, no matter the level of resistance. Another journey on a straight line in defiance of physics appears in a story he tells Randolph about a trip to the moon. "I fell asleep in a ski lift, went past my stop and woke upright in the middle of what's-his-name's crater" (76). And doesn't the narrator promise God that "I will find You one day, and when I do, I'll straighten Your spiral for You and tie a knot in it as well"?

Allowing, then, that the narrator succeeds in unseating God and that the novel takes place in an unspecified (again, as in Poe) time but more or less contemporaneous to its composition, then since that time the universe must have been in his/His hands. Though this Borgesian or Dickian concept I find imaginatively appealing, I haven't noticed much difference since the regime change in Heaven or heard of a new Leonardo on the market. Perhaps he becomes God and of the world changes only what is necessary to write himself into a fiction. On the other hand (if it is the other hand), assuming the narrator took his madness with him into the other world, need there have been much of if any difference between the time before and after Alfred Omega's coronation?

My preferred choice, each time I read *It Happened in Boston?* is that, within the universe of possibilities that constitute this, as the first edition's front cover judiciously has it, extraordinary novel, the narrator is crowned God. That I tend toward the narrator's ultimate success in spite of the more logical conclusion that he's simply a captured madman is due in part to Greenan's (as he will in his other first-person novels) making a madman, psychopath, and murderer sympathetic, in part to my wanting to acknowledge the novel's artful edifice by grounding my reading in the textual clues discussed above (and radiant throughout the novel) and thus grant Greenan's narrator a role to play in the comedy's creation.

A black comedy, I hope it's now clear, as bitter at times as Nathanael West, as cinereous with ambiguity as Pynchon. Oedipa Maas, a slightly older cousin of the narrator of *It Happened in Boston?* on her Quest for "the direct, epileptic Word" (118) is also caught in her author's web of paranoia. Everything connects, so nothing does. In a meaningless universe everything means, and more than twice. ("Everyone here seems to be at *least* a double agent" [*Gravity's Rainbow* 632]). And revelation is always just out of reach.

Or perhaps my somewhat lunatic reading of *It Happened in Boston?* comes from my desiring, simply, that the narrator and all of us never be deceived by the Deity, that ultimate creation, Supreme Prince of Condom and Generator of the unknown, again.

CODA:

REFLECTIONS ON THE LITERARY CAREER OF RUSSELL H. GREENAN

I first taught Russell H. Greenan's *It Happened in Boston?* in 1971–72 at St. Maria Goretti High School in Lake Arthur, a small southwest Louisiana town about fifteen miles south of Jennings, forty east of Lake Charles, forty from the Gulf—a great place to teach a novel about an artist who wants a meeting with God in order to kill Him. St. Maria Goretti School was one of those two-story cardboard constructions you assume will blow away in a big wind. On Ash Wednesday, the students—in their khaki shirts and slacks (boys) or white blouses and navy blue skirts (girls)—walked around with large black crosses marked on their foreheads by Father Soileau earlier that morning at Mass. Reading *It Happened in Boston?* was a revelation of a different sort to my students at St. Maria Goretti. In my classroom on the second floor, with its picture of JFK on the back wall and beside the blackboard a statue of Jesus (upon which on my more blasphemous days—I was twenty-two years old—I hung my jacket), I observed for the first time the delight students found in a careful reading of Greenan's first novel.

A few years and jobs later I was teaching the novel again at the New Orleans Center for Creative Arts and continued to do so there over the next three decades. The year the Tutankhamen exhibit came to the New Orleans Museum of Art, I and my class read in place of *Boston? The Secret Life of Algernon Pendleton* whose likeable albeit homicidal narrator lives off selling some of the Egyptian artifacts acquired by his grandfather, a famous Egyptologist. I recall our discussing Algernon's metaphysics under an oak tree in City Park after we had just toured the exhibit.

High school classes, undergraduate, graduate, no matter the level or state or country, I was always asked: "Why isn't there more written on Greenan? Why are his books out of print?" A good question, but haven't there always been, as literary history amply demonstrates, more writers of exceptional work worthy of our attention than most arbiters and marketers of literature care to admit? And then, who finally can explain why authors B and Y are enshrined, while Z and A, greater in every conceivable sense, are forgotten?

For decades I praised Greenan's work to whomever I could, prowled used bookstores in the US and Europe in search of spare copies of his novels to pass along to friends. In London's now-deceased Murder One on Charing Cross, a canted copy of *The Bric-a-Brac Man*; in a Goodwill on Maryland's Eastern Shore, a tattered *Queen of America*; hours shifting paper sacks filled with paperbacks in The Olive Tree on Royal Street in New Orleans to uncover another copy of *It Happened in Boston?* In my NOCCA classroom (Rm. 204, 6048 Perrier) I stored my extras of *Boston?* and *Pendleton* in a large old wooden cabinet with glass doors, the extent of my horde ever visible. Eventually I ran out of copies of *Pendleton* to teach, but never of the first three editions of *Boston?*

Published when its author was forty-three, *It Happened in Boston?* was vigorously promoted by Random House. Most reviews were raves. "On all counts Russell Greenan has written a superbly macabre and satisfying novel. The details are grisly, the people lunatic, but the results are magnetic," said the *New York Times*, and *United Press International* called Greenan "a born novelist." The author of *It Happened in Boston?* had "the mind of a sorcerer and his book is magical." The Literary Guild brought out a book club edition (orange paper boards, instead of the publisher's black cloth), and Fawcett Crest paid $100,000 for the paperback rights, making Greenan's gamble to move himself and his family to Nice for a year to write the novel a smart one.

Visibility the book had. When in February 1969, as an English major at the University of Arkansas, Fayetteville, I read the review in *Time* ("With painterly sleight of hand, he recreates the fabulous landscape of a deranged artist's mind. It is a terrain at once fearful and frolicsome—as if Breughel's earthy dancing peasantry had been set down in a demon-filled scene by Hieronymus Bosch"), I promised myself I would purchase the paperback. A novel about a painter who aspires to unseat God and murders seven people for the chance—yes, I wouldn't forget to look for the affordable paperback of *It Happened in Boston?*

After four different covers from American publishers,[42] the 1970 Fawcett Crest paperback is the one I see first in my mind's eye. The title and author are centered at the top in black script against a white background. Centered below in midground stands a young man in dark brown slacks, light brown jacket, white shirt, no tie, stretching his left arm to the sky. On his raised hand he holds a hand-puppet frog whose head effaces the bottom part of the *t* in *Boston?* To the man's left (frame right) a young woman with long black hair wearing a wine-red gown, her face in partial profile, gazes behind him. The man stares upward, even his hair points to the sky, as if blown by a wind from below. His right arm is in front of him, perhaps

42 The covers of all of Greenan's novels in English and translation can be found at http://www.russellhgreenan.info

to ward off the pigeon in the foreground (bottom left), its wings spread in flight. And there's one further fortuitous crowning touch to the cover: in the top right-hand corner, above the 95¢ price, the Fawcett Crest gold crown emblem, as if in recognition of the crown in the novel's finale that's placed on the head of the narrator.

When half a year after reading *Boston?* I came across the hardback of Greenan's second novel *Nightmare* in a bookstore in Roanoke, Virginia, I bought it at once, amazed at my good fortune to have found a new novel by the author of *It Happened in Boston?* The cover was black, the author's photo on the back the same as on his previous work, and in orange letters the front cover announced the book as "A Contemporary Tale of Horror." Well, yes, but then readers expecting the usual horror decor and narrative design risked being disappointed, and those after more "literary" fare missed out. I read of Steven Pierglass's ordeal in a New York City boarding house in my upstairs apartment that fall in Mrs. Peck's farmhouse outside Fincastle, Virginia, between readings of Barthelme's *Snow White* and Beckett's *Stories and Texts for Nothing*, also in their own way metaphysical horror comedies. Though *Boston?* was more widely reviewed, *Nightmare* was still well received: "memorable divergence from the beaten suspense trail"; "the horrors of race and deprivation and pointless death and madness reflect on all humanity" (*New York Times Book Review*); "at a time when so many white writers are using the black struggle as a basis for pretentious, ill-conceived, and self-serving fiction, Mr. Greenan's perspective and taste make him a welcome exception" (*Washington Post Book World*).

The front cover of Greenan's next novel, *The Queen of America* (1972), as I continue to trace lightly his career, baldly called this dark comic satire of America "A Horror Story." Though the quality of production wasn't up to the standards of the first two books (paper, not cloth boards, glue binding), one can understand Random House's dilemma. The *New York Times* alluded to the difficulty of categorizing Greenan's novels in its April 2, 1972 review: "This is a hard book to describe, but it exerts an uncanny fascination, is brilliantly written, and has characters who will not easily leave the mind."

Paperback editions of both *Nightmare* and *The Queen of America* were brought out by Warner Books in 1972 and 1973. The cover for the latter shows a bell-bottomed blond on a motorcycle wielding in her right hand a scythe. Despite the favorable reviews of the novel and Greenan's previous two, Warner Books decided against high-end marketing and used no reviewer blurbs on or within the covers. Besides the author and title, the front cover says only: "MEET MISS PSYCHO—SHE'S THE SHOCK EXPERIENCE OF YOUR LIFE! A HORROR STORY BY THE AUTHOR OF IT HAPPENED IN BOSTON?" while the back cover informs us "BETSY WILL STEAL YOUR HEART EVEN IF SHE HAS TO USE A KNIFE. She seemed to be just another young hippy, traveling across the States on a battered bike, looking for kicks. But Betsy's favorite idea of a good time was hacking innocent people to death—and then taking them apart, piece by bloody piece. And no one had ever found a way to cramp the cold-blooded life of THE QUEEN OF AMERICA." Good readers need to read between the lines of a book's marketing, but how exactly are they to do this? How to see in Warner Books' description of the novel as "The Ultimate Trip Into Ultra-Terror" a novel about America whose lineage drew from the tradition of both Hawthorne and Twain?

Greenan's fourth novel, *The Secret Life of Algernon Pendleton* (1973) was, thankfully, left unclassified, though *Publisher's Weekly* called it a "sort of *Arsenic and Old Lace* . . . A fanciful blend of madness and murder in which the outrageous and unbelievable are treated as naturally as if they were everyday occurrences." The novel was better promoted than the previous two and next to *Boston?* his most widely reviewed and praised. O. L. Bailey in *Saturday Review* noted its "echoes" to "early Waugh and other parts of the literary landscape from Graham Greene to John Fowles" and that "Greenan [had] fashioned an excursion into the macabre that is in a class by itself." The Fawcett Crest (sans crown) paperback is the edition I taught from.

Of his two remaining novels published with Random House, *Heart of Gold* ("A Melodrama") and *The Bric-a-Brac Man* ("An Extravaganza"), in 1975 and 1976 respectively, only the former appeared in paperback (Fawcett Crest). Reviewing *Heart of Gold* in the *New York Times*, Christopher Lehmann-Haupt said that "[w]hat Mr. Greenan does well he does better than ever in the latest in a series of charming gothic tales." And of *The Bric-a-Brac Man* he wrote: "I get the feeling that through some oversight or taxonomical confusion (Mr. Greenan's books are difficult to classify, therefore hard to explain), not enough readers are aware of what delightful fun he is poking at the notion that human beings are superior to skunk cabbages." On the 1976 Fawcett Crest paperback edition of *Heart of Gold* not a single quote from the reviews appear, nor a blurb by a fellow practictioner, nor quotes from earlier reviews. A handsome paperback, in gold and black, but a reader new to Greenan would assume the novel went unreviewed, or if reviewed then unfavorably.

The Bric-a-Brac Man was the last novel Greenan published in hardback with Random House. His next novel, *Keepers* (1978), was brought out by St. Martin's and went mostly unnoticed by the major newspapers, nor did it receive a paperback reprint. And then, after publishing seven brilliantly conceived macabre comedies, there came a ten-year drought for his English-language readers.

When he surfaced again it was in 1987 with a paperback original, *A Can of Worms*, which Bantam brought out simultaneously with new editions of *It Happened in Boston?* and *The Secret Life of*

Algernon Pendleton.[43] For a paperback original, the novel was surprisingly well received, though not this time by Lehmann-Haupt whose notice in the *New York Times* found "a mean-spiritedness" in it he hadn't seen in Greenan's work before. On the other hand, writing in the *Washington Post Book World*, Michele Slung stated in her first sentence: "There is something wrong with a world in which Russell Greenan is not a household name" and went on to say that the novel "is about as good as it gets: I'd almost go so far as to call it a small masterpiece." But paperbacks have abbreviated shelf lives, and by the time some of the reviews appeared, *A Can of Worms* was probably already off the rack, its front cover ripped off, and the remains pulped. Greenan, unlike crime writers such as Jim Thompson, David Goodis, or Charles Willeford, was never stuck in the publishing ghetto of paperback originals, so he never had the chance to be lifted out of it.

Between 1987 and 2003, when Random House reprinted *It Happened in Boston?* no new edition of a book by Russell H. Greenan appeared in English.

In France, however, his first eight novels were published (out of sequence) from 1971 to 2004, with *Nightmare* (his second novel) appearing first and *The Queen of America* (his third novel) last, as well as two novels that have yet to find English-language publishers, *La Nuit du jugement dernier/Doomsnight* (1990) and *Magique Micmac/Glamour Doom* (2002). These two novels and a third, *Dread of Night* which appeared in the US at the end of 2009, are

43 Bantam also announced an edition of *Heart of Gold*, but it never appeared, due I assume to insufficient sales from the other three titles. David Ulin, in his review in *Bookforum* of the 2003 reprint of *Boston?* "God Damns Him," recalls being dismayed by Bantam's marketing of Greenan's "disquieting little masterpiece" of "metaphysical retribution" as a crime novel.

remarkable performances, perfectly plotted, screamingly funny, and moral to their core. They pick up the major themes, motifs, and techniques of his earlier work and expand them—in the case of *Dread of Night* like a mushroom cloud over the globe.[44]

In "A Conversation with Russell H. Greenan," Greenan described the novels *Doomsnight* and *Dread of Night* as "stark, hard-edged tales dealing with terrorism. The third, *Glamour Doom*, is a story about, among other things, a woman who may or may not have the power to cause people she dislikes to suffer grave misfortunes. Since I was born in 1925," he added, "I grew up in the thirties and forties, a period far less forbearing than today, and the characters and situations in these later books (written by an older man, it must be pointed out as well) reflect that background." Regarding the lack of an English-language publisher for *Doomsnight* and *Glamour Doom*, he said: "The French, though they are open to a very broad range of writing, have a particular passion for noir, so these dark stories appeal to them. *IHiB?* my first book, was not the first to be printed there. It was the fifth."

In a recent letter (November 2009) Greenan told me he wrote two other novels, LITERARY LICENSE (1982), "which was lost in Florida," and ANOTHER LOVE STORY (1989). Of these works I know only their titles.

Eleven (of thirteen) novels published in forty years, some interest from the film business,[45] translations of his books into Dutch,

---

44 *Glamour Doom* was copyrighted by the author in 1993 but did not appear in French until 2002. In 2006 Greenan completed "a shortened rendition" of *Doomsnight* which is the version I read. *Dread of Night* was under consideration with Random House when the 9/11 attack on the US occurred and turned down two days later. (Private correspondence)

45 Including a film based on *The Secret Life of Algernon Pendleton*, *The Secret Life of Algernon* (1997), directed by Charles Jarrott (*The Amateur*, 1982), which

German, Spanish, French, and Italian in over forty different editions—not at all a bad career, a very good one, in fact, though not what most would consider wildly successful. At least that's how this observer sees Greenan's career in broad outline.

Why hasn't Greenan been more feted? In large part, as I've suggested, this is due to the difficulty in categorizing his books, of selecting the right taxonomical tag to clip onto them. Greenan, as I noted in the introduction, "would not have been surprised" had his "offbeat tale" *It Happened in Boston?* gone unpublished (2003, 281). Greenan's preferred genre, no matter how many categories we couple together like train cars (crime-horror-gothic-comedy-melodrama-theological-fantasy-noir-extravaganza-Arabesque), is his own. If a single category applied or had he decided to write to specification, his career would have been different, but I suspect his books might have lost much of their originality and edginess.

Beyond the problem of how to classify his dark baroque entertainments, his erudite grotesques, his charmingly disruptive comedies, lies his uncompromising vision. Greenan is more immediately entertaining than Céline, whose work he acknowledged as an influence, and at the same time just as dark, if not more so. At its best, Greenan's work is as bleakly brilliant and perceptive about *Homo Americanus* as West's *Day of the Locust* or Hammett's *Red Harvest*. Not that I don't understand a publisher's timidity when confronted with an outrageous masterwork like *Dread of Night*. What editor could believe readers would enjoy a novel that begins with flower pots as a murder weapon and ends after homegrown

---

won a couple of awards and vanished without a wide release. I know of at least three screenplays based on *Boston?* Greenan wrote to me that a French producer had optioned *Heart of Gold*, "but then abandoned the project because he felt my homicidal minister might offend his audience." And in another letter: "The only real money I ever made out of writing came from film producers—many options, and three outright sales."

atomic bombs have destroyed several US cities? Only the rare (or extinct?) editor could accept that a satire this pointed, deadly, and smart might not only be fun to read but also right for our times.

What kept academia from taking up Greenan? For one thing, arriving on the scene in the late sixties although a child of the 1920s and 1930s, Greenan did not fall in line with the postmodernists. Although one can find the occasional reflexive gesture, Greenan's work more clearly derives from a character- and plot-driven axis than an experimental or reflexive one. And why not? The fiction Greenan fed on in his youth ("*The Postman Always Rings Twice* and *Double Indemnity* were revelations to me sixty-five years ago"; "There was a time when I probably could have recited *The Maltese Falcon* verbatim from memory"[46]) didn't need to ironize the world; life *was* already sufficiently ironic. The miracle, or one of the miracles, of Greenan's career is how his agent managed to find publishers for his black comedies. That academics failed to catch on is no surprise. Novels considered horror (Shirley Jackson's *We Have Always Lived in the Castle* [1962]) or crime (Thompson's *The Killer Inside Me* [1952]) or science fiction (Dick's *Martian Time-Slip* [1964]) or western (Willeford's *The Difference* [1971/1999]) academics had yet to deem worthy of serious attention.

One might say his publishers did their best, and not without some success, though one can also easily imagine Dantean levels of corporate incompetence as a likely culprit for the fact that most of Greenan's books are currently out of print. And then there are the odds, simply. There are lots of writers out there, even more books, and sometimes the best of them (the novels of Stephen Becker are another example) are overlooked. Good Luck versus Bad Luck. Or: No Luck At All. Sales figures tell the (bottom-line) tale, of course, and modest sales are never welcomed. The book

46 Private correspondence.

is packaged, promoted (or not), sold (or not). A flurry of reviews or a trickle. And then, too often, silence, indifference, the death of a career.

Which I'm pleased to say is not the case with Russell H. Greenan's. Nor, I suspect, will it ever be. Four US editions of *Boston?* with reassessments by Anne Tyler in the *Washington Post Book World* in 1982 ("Apart from its originality and complexity, it has that most exhilarating of qualities: the power to rewaken our sense of life's possibilities") and Jonathan Lethem in 2003 ("Russell Greenan's *It Happened in Boston?* is a magic spell of a book" [x]). There are several reasons why the novel keeps coming back into print, and not the least of them can be found in Greenan's straightforward aesthetic: "I try to write believable novels with original plots and characters" ("Conversation").

Whether mad, murderous or minor, Greenan's characters, like his plots, are always vividly entertaining, and his style a lesson in music, metaphor, and precision, as in this example from *The Secret Life of Algernon Pendleto*n when Al is surprised by the crying, the "resonant *roomph-roomph-roomph*, repeated with metronomic regularity" of Norbie Hess, his fat, frog-like friend who saved his life after their ship was shelled during WWII (and whom Al later will murder):

> Norbie was seated in the quilted chair. He was dressed in a bright Hawaiian shirt and a capacious pair of taupe Bermuda shorts. Down his broad, puffy face, great tears streamed. With each *roomph-roomph* his chest heaved as though he were undergoing a severe convulsion, and the flowered shirt went up and down like a meadow in an earthquake. For an instant I supposed that he was ill; then

> he wiped his eyes with a soggy handkerchief and shook his head sorrowfully, and I recognized that he was simply crying . . .
>
> As the lugubrious sound filled the house, I fled out the back door and went to sit in the Burying Ground. It was a fine day. The rich-blue sky was speckled with ragged swatches of white clouds that looked like exploding antiaircraft shells. In the stand of oaks, some jays were whistling. A faint echo of their calls reverberated from the office buildings on Carlton Street. (52–53)

Buried in the sky of this graveyard scene, among other manifestations of Greenan's art, are figurative antiaircraft shells echoing Algernon's war experience and brain injury. And those "ragged swatches" of clouds (like cerecloth?) point us to Al's (mystical? mental?) encounter with a frog on Hall's Pond near the novel's end. "Ragged! Ragged!" croaks this perceptive amphibian, "ragged hazard" (211–12).

As long as there are readers who don't mind hearing a few jokes while dangling over the abyss, the novels of Russell H. Greenan will not be forgotten.

BIBLIOGRAPHY

Bailey, O. L. Review of *The Secret Life of Algernon Pendleton. The Saturday Review*, 1973.

Barthes, Roland. *The Pleasure of the Text*. Tr. Richard Miller. New York: Farrar, Straus and Giroux, 1975.

Beckett, Samuel. *Mercier and Camier*. New York: Grove Press, 1975.

—. *Molloy, Malone Dies, The Unnamable*. New York: Knopf, 1997.

—. *Waiting for Godot*. New York: Grove Press, 1954.

Blackburn, Sara. "Growing to Know." Review of *Nightmare*. *Washington Post Book World* (Dec. 12, 1970).

Calasso, Roberto. *Literature and the Gods*. New York: Knopf, 2001.

Callender, Newgate. "Criminals at Large." Review of *The Queen of America*. *New York Times Book Review* (Apr. 9, 1972).

De Quincey, Thomas. *Joan of Arc and The English Mail Coach*. New York: Charles E. Merrill Co., 1906.

Dick, Philip K. *The Transmigration of Timothy Archer*. New York: Timescape Book, 1982.

Dickens, Charles. *David Copperfield*. New York: Signet, 1962.

Dostoevsky, Fyodor. *The Brothers Karamazov*. Tr. Richard Peaver and Larissa Volokhonsky. New York: Vintage, 1991.

Feuerbach, Ludwig. "God as a Projection of the Human Mind." Tr. George Eliot. In *The Existence of God*, ed. John Hick. New York: Macmillan, 1964: 191-204.

Foucault, Michel. *Death and the Labyrinth: The World of Raymond Roussel*. Tr. Charles Ruas. Garden City: Doubleday, 1986.

—. *Madness and Civilization: A History of Insanity in the Age of Reason*. New York: Vintage, 1988.

Gogol, Nikolai. *The Diary of a Madman and Other Stories*. Tr. Andrew R. MacAndrew. New York: Signet, 1960.

Greenan, Russell H. *It Happened in Boston?* New York: Random House, 1968.

—. *It Happened in Boston?* Greenwich: Fawcett Crest, 1970.

—. *It Happened in Boston?* New York: Bantam Books, 1987.

—. *It Happened in Boston?* Intr. Jonathan Lethem, Afterword by the author. New York: Modern Library, 2003.

—. *Nightmare*. New York: Random House, 1970.

—. *Nightmare*. New York: Warner Books, 1972.

—. *The Queen of America*. New York: Random House, 1972.

—. *The Queen of America*. New York: Warner Books, 1973.

—. *The Secret Life of Algernon Pendleton*. New York: Random House, 1973.

—. *The Secret Life of Algernon Pendleton*. Greenwich: Fawcett Crest, 1974.

—. *The Secret Life of Algernon Pendleton*. New York: Bantam Books, 1988.

—. *Heart of Gold*. New York: Random House, 1975.

—. *Heart of Gold*. Greenwich: Fawcett Crest, 1976.

—. *The Bric-a-Brac Man*. New York: Random House, 1976.

—. *Keepers*. New York: St. Martin's Press, 1978.

—. *A Can of Worms*. New York: Bantam, 1987.

—. *La Nuit du jugement dernier*. Tr. Marie-Françoise Husson. Paris: Rivages, 1996.

—. *Magique micmac*. Tr. Aurélie Tronchet. Paris: Murder Inc., 2002.

—. "A Conversation with Russell H. Greenan." Random House/The Modern Library (www.randomhouse.com/modernlibrary/Greenan.html), 2003.

—. *Dread of Night*. Daemonax Books, 2009.

—. http://www.russellhgreenan.info

Hamburger, Michael. *Contraries: Studies in German Literature*. New York: E.P. Dutton, 1970.

Harrison, William. *The Theologian*. New York: Harper & Row, 1965.

Hawthorne, Nathaniel. *The Elixir of Life Manuscripts*. Colombus: Ohio State University Press, 1977.

—. *The House of the Seven Gables*. Ed. Milton R. Stern. New York: Penguin, 1986.

Hoffman, Daniel. *Poe Poe Poe Poe Poe Poe Poe*. New York: Avon, 1978.

Hubin, Allen J. "Criminals at Large." Review of *Nightmare*. *New York Times Book Review* (July 12, 1970).

James, William. *The Varieties of Religious Experience*. New York: Signet, 2003.

Jung, C. G. *Four Archetypes: Mother/Rebirth/Spirit/Trickster*. Tr. R. F. C. Hull. Princeton: Princeton University Press, 1970.

Kazin, Alfred. *God and the American Writer*. New York: Vintage, 1998.

Lask, Thomas. Review of *It Happened in Boston? New York Times* (Feb. 5, 1969).

Lehmann-Haupt, Christopher. Review of *Heart of Gold*. *New York Times* (Mar. 14, 1978).

—. Review of *The Bric-a-Brac Man. New York Times* (Nov. 5, 1976).
—. Review of *A Can of Worms. New York Times* (July 25,1987).
Levin, Harry. *The Power of Blackness: Hawthorne, Poe, Melville.* New York: Vintage, 1958.
McElroy, Bernard. *Fiction of the Modern Grotesque.* New York: St. Martin's Press, 1989.
Melville, Herman. *The Confidence-Man: His Masquerade.* Afterword by R.W. B. Lewis. New York: Signet, 1964.
—. *Moby-Dick; or, The Whale.* New York: Penguin, 1992.
—. *The Piazza Tales and Other Prose Pieces 1839–1860.* Evanston and Chicago: Northwestern University Press and Newberry Library, 1987.
Nabokov, Vladimir. *The Gift.* New York: Vintage, 1991.
—. *Lectures on Literature.* New York: Harcourt Brace Jovanovich, 1980.
—. *Lolita.* New York: Putnam, 1958.
Poe, Edgar Allan. *Complete Tales and Poems.* New York: Vintage, 1975.
—. *Eureka, A Prose Poem.* Los Angeles: Green Integer, 1997.
—. *The Fall of the House of Usher and Other Writings.* London: Penguin, 1986.
Pynchon, Thomas. *The Crying of Lot 49.* New York: Harper Perennial, 1986.
—. *Gravity's Rainbow.* New York: Bantam, 1974.
Rorty, Richard. *The Barber of Kasbeam: Nabokov on Cruelty.* Bennington: The Bennington Chapbooks in Literature, 1988.
Queneau, Raymond. *Zazie.* Tr. Barbara Wright. New York: Harper & Brothers, 1960.
Slung, Michele. "Murder Most Mordant." Review of *A Can of Worms. Washington Post Book World* (Aug. 10, 1987).

Thompson, Jim. *After Dark, My Sweet*. Berkeley: Black Lizard Books, 1985.

—. *Pop. 1280*. New York: Vintage/Black Lizard, 1990.

Time Magazine. "Dreams of Disorder." Review of *It Happened in Boston?* Feb. 7, 1969.

Tyler, Anne. "Flights of Fancy, Planes of Reality." *Washington Post Book World* (June 27, 1982).

Twain, Mark. *Adventures of Huckleberry Finn*. Scranton, Pa.: Chandler Publishing Company, 1962.

Ulin, David. "God Damns Him." *Review of It Happened in Boston? Bookforum* (Fall, 2003).

Wadlington, Warwick. *The Confidence Game in American Literature*. Princeton: Princeton University Press, 1975.

Walser, Robert. *Selected Stories*. Tr. Christopher Middleton and others. New York: New York Review Books, 2002.

Waugh, Evelyn. *A Handful of Dust*. London: Penguin, 1951.

Winters, Yvor. *In Defense of Reason*. New York: Swallow Press and William Morrow, 1947.

TOM WHALEN is a novelist, poet, translator and author of numerous stories and critical essays. He has written for *Agni, Bookforum, Film Quarterly, The Hopkins Review, The Iowa Review, The Literary Review, Studies in Short Fiction, The Wallace Stevens Journal,* the *Washington Post*, and other publications, and he co-edited the *Review of Contemporary Fiction*'s "Robert Walser Number."

SELECTED DALKEY ARCHIVE PAPERBACKS

PETROS ABATZOGLOU, *What Does Mrs. Freeman Want?*
MICHAL AJVAZ, *The Golden Age.*
The Other City.
PIERRE ALBERT-BIROT, *Grabinoulor.*
YUZ ALESHKOVSKY, *Kangaroo.*
FELIPE ALFAU, *Chromos.*
Locos.
IVAN ÂNGELO, *The Celebration.*
The Tower of Glass.
DAVID ANTIN, *Talking.*
ANTÓNIO LOBO ANTUNES, *Knowledge of Hell.*
ALAIN ARIAS-MISSON, *Theatre of Incest.*
IFTIKHAR ARIF AND WAQAS KHWAJA, EDS., *Modern Poetry of Pakistan.*
JOHN ASHBERY AND JAMES SCHUYLER, *A Nest of Ninnies.*
GABRIELA AVIGUR-ROTEM, *Heatwave and Crazy Birds.*
HEIMRAD BÄCKER, *transcript.*
DJUNA BARNES, *Ladies Almanack.*
Ryder.
JOHN BARTH, *LETTERS.*
Sabbatical.
DONALD BARTHELME, *The King.*
Paradise.
SVETISLAV BASARA, *Chinese Letter.*
RENÉ BELLETTO, *Dying.*
MARK BINELLI, *Sacco and Vanzetti Must Die!*
ANDREI BITOV, *Pushkin House.*
ANDREJ BLATNIK, *You Do Understand.*
LOUIS PAUL BOON, *Chapel Road.*
My Little War.
Summer in Termuren.
ROGER BOYLAN, *Killoyle.*
IGNÁCIO DE LOYOLA BRANDÃO, *Anonymous Celebrity.*
The Good-Bye Angel.
Teeth under the Sun.
Zero.
BONNIE BREMSER, *Troia: Mexican Memoirs.*
CHRISTINE BROOKE-ROSE, *Amalgamemnon.*
BRIGID BROPHY, *In Transit.*
MEREDITH BROSNAN, *Mr. Dynamite.*
GERALD L. BRUNS, *Modern Poetry and the Idea of Language.*
EVGENY BUNIMOVICH AND J. KATES, EDS., *Contemporary Russian Poetry: An Anthology.*
GABRIELLE BURTON, *Heartbreak Hotel.*
MICHEL BUTOR, *Degrees.*
Mobile.
Portrait of the Artist as a Young Ape.
G. CABRERA INFANTE, *Infante's Inferno.*
Three Trapped Tigers.
JULIETA CAMPOS, *The Fear of Losing Eurydice.*
ANNE CARSON, *Eros the Bittersweet.*
ORLY CASTEL-BLOOM, *Dolly City.*
CAMILO JOSÉ CELA, *Christ versus Arizona.*
The Family of Pascual Duarte.
The Hive.
LOUIS-FERDINAND CÉLINE, *Castle to Castle.*
Conversations with Professor Y.
London Bridge.
Normance.
North.
Rigadoon.
HUGO CHARTERIS, *The Tide Is Right.*
JEROME CHARYN, *The Tar Baby.*
ERIC CHEVILLARD, *Demolishing Nisard.*
MARC CHOLODENKO, *Mordechai Schamz.*
JOSHUA COHEN, *Witz.*
EMILY HOLMES COLEMAN, *The Shutter of Snow.*
ROBERT COOVER, *A Night at the Movies.*
STANLEY CRAWFORD, *Log of the S.S. The Mrs Unguentine.*
Some Instructions to My Wife.
ROBERT CREELEY, *Collected Prose.*
RENÉ CREVEL, *Putting My Foot in It.*
RALPH CUSACK, *Cadenza.*
SUSAN DAITCH, *L.C.*
Storytown.
NICHOLAS DELBANCO, *The Count of Concord.*
Sherbrookes.
NIGEL DENNIS, *Cards of Identity.*
PETER DIMOCK, *A Short Rhetoric for Leaving the Family.*
ARIEL DORFMAN, *Konfidenz.*
COLEMAN DOWELL, *The Houses of Children.*
Island People.
Too Much Flesh and Jabez.
ARKADII DRAGOMOSHCHENKO, *Dust.*
RIKKI DUCORNET, *The Complete Butcher's Tales.*
The Fountains of Neptune.
The Jade Cabinet.
The One Marvelous Thing.
Phosphor in Dreamland.
The Stain.
The Word "Desire."
WILLIAM EASTLAKE, *The Bamboo Bed.*
Castle Keep.
Lyric of the Circle Heart.
JEAN ECHENOZ, *Chopin's Move.*
STANLEY ELKIN, *A Bad Man.*
Boswell: A Modern Comedy.
Criers and Kibitzers, Kibitzers and Criers.
The Dick Gibson Show.
The Franchiser.
George Mills.
The Living End.
The MacGuffin.
The Magic Kingdom.
Mrs. Ted Bliss.
The Rabbi of Lud.
Van Gogh's Room at Arles.
ANNIE ERNAUX, *Cleaned Out.*
LAUREN FAIRBANKS, *Muzzle Thyself.*
Sister Carrie.
LESLIE A. FIEDLER, *Love and Death in the American Novel.*
JUAN FILLOY, *Op Oloop.*
GUSTAVE FLAUBERT, *Bouvard and Pécuchet.*
KASS FLEISHER, *Talking out of School.*
FORD MADOX FORD, *The March of Literature.*
JON FOSSE, *Aliss at the Fire.*
Melancholy.
MAX FRISCH, *I'm Not Stiller.*
Man in the Holocene.

SELECTED DALKEY ARCHIVE PAPERBACKS

Carlos Fuentes, *Christopher Unborn.*
Distant Relations.
Terra Nostra.
Where the Air Is Clear.
Janice Galloway, *Foreign Parts.*
The Trick Is to Keep Breathing.
William H. Gass, *Cartesian Sonata and Other Novellas.*
Finding a Form.
A Temple of Texts.
The Tunnel.
Willie Masters' Lonesome Wife.
Gérard Gavarry, *Hoppla! 1 2 3.*
Making a Novel.
Etienne Gilson,
The Arts of the Beautiful.
Forms and Substances in the Arts.
C. S. Giscombe, *Giscome Road.*
Here.
Prairie Style.
Douglas Glover, *Bad News of the Heart.*
The Enamoured Knight.
Witold Gombrowicz,
A Kind of Testament.
Karen Elizabeth Gordon,
The Red Shoes.
Georgi Gospodinov, *Natural Novel.*
Juan Goytisolo, *Count Julian.*
Exiled from Almost Everywhere.
Juan the Landless.
Makbara.
Marks of Identity.
Patrick Grainville, *The Cave of Heaven.*
Henry Green, *Back.*
Blindness.
Concluding.
Doting.
Nothing.
Jiří Gruša, *The Questionnaire.*
Gabriel Gudding,
Rhode Island Notebook.
Mela Hartwig, *Am I a Redundant Human Being?*
John Hawkes, *The Passion Artist.*
Whistlejacket.
Aleksandar Hemon, ed.,
Best European Fiction.
Aidan Higgins, *A Bestiary.*
Balcony of Europe.
Bornholm Night-Ferry.
Darkling Plain: Texts for the Air.
Flotsam and Jetsam.
Langrishe, Go Down.
Scenes from a Receding Past.
Windy Arbours.
Keizo Hino, *Isle of Dreams.*
Kazushi Hosaka, *Plainsong.*
Aldous Huxley, *Antic Hay.*
Crome Yellow.
Point Counter Point.
Those Barren Leaves.
Time Must Have a Stop.
Naoyuki Ii, *The Shadow of a Blue Cat.*
Mikhail Iossel and Jeff Parker, eds.,
Amerika: Russian Writers View the United States.
Gert Jonke, *The Distant Sound.*
Geometric Regional Novel.
Homage to Czerny.
The System of Vienna.
Jacques Jouet, *Mountain R.*
Savage.
Upstaged.
Charles Juliet, *Conversations with Samuel Beckett and Bram van Velde.*
Mieko Kanai, *The Word Book.*
Yoram Kaniuk, *Life on Sandpaper.*
Hugh Kenner, *The Counterfeiters.*
Flaubert, Joyce and Beckett: The Stoic Comedians.
Joyce's Voices.
Danilo Kiš, *Garden, Ashes.*
A Tomb for Boris Davidovich.
Anita Konkka, *A Fool's Paradise.*
George Konrád, *The City Builder.*
Tadeusz Konwicki, *A Minor Apocalypse.*
The Polish Complex.
Menis Koumandareas, *Koula.*
Elaine Kraf, *The Princess of 72nd Street.*
Jim Krusoe, *Iceland.*
Ewa Kuryluk, *Century 21.*
Emilio Lascano Tegui, *On Elegance While Sleeping.*
Eric Laurrent, *Do Not Touch.*
Hervé Le Tellier, *The Sextine Chapel.*
A Thousand Pearls (for a Thousand Pennies)
Violette Leduc, *La Bâtarde.*
Edouard Levé, *Suicide.*
Suzanne Jill Levine, *The Subversive Scribe: Translating Latin American Fiction.*
Deborah Levy, *Billy and Girl.*
Pillow Talk in Europe and Other Places.
José Lezama Lima, *Paradiso.*
Rosa Liksom, *Dark Paradise.*
Osman Lins, *Avalovara.*
The Queen of the Prisons of Greece.
Alf Mac Lochlainn,
The Corpus in the Library.
Out of Focus.
Ron Loewinsohn, *Magnetic Field(s).*
Mina Loy, *Stories and Essays of Mina Loy.*
Brian Lynch, *The Winner of Sorrow.*
D. Keith Mano, *Take Five.*
Micheline Aharonian Marcom,
The Mirror in the Well.
Ben Marcus,
The Age of Wire and String.
Wallace Markfield,
Teitlebaum's Window.
To an Early Grave.
David Markson, *Reader's Block.*
Springer's Progress.
Wittgenstein's Mistress.
Carole Maso, *AVA.*
Ladislav Matejka and Krystyna Pomorska, eds.,
Readings in Russian Poetics: Formalist and Structuralist Views.
Harry Mathews,
The Case of the Persevering Maltese: Collected Essays.
Cigarettes.
The Conversions.
The Human Country: New and Collected Stories.
The Journalist.

FOR A FULL LIST OF PUBLICATIONS, VISIT:
www.dalkeyarchive.com

SELECTED DALKEY ARCHIVE PAPERBACKS

ARNO SCHMIDT, *Collected Novellas.*
Collected Stories.
Nobodaddy's Children.
Two Novels.
ASAF SCHURR, *Motti.*
CHRISTINE SCHUTT, *Nightwork.*
GAIL SCOTT, *My Paris.*
DAMION SEARLS, *What We Were Doing and Where We Were Going.*
JUNE AKERS SEESE,
Is This What Other Women Feel Too?
What Waiting Really Means.
BERNARD SHARE, *Inish.*
Transit.
AURELIE SHEEHAN,
Jack Kerouac Is Pregnant.
VIKTOR SHKLOVSKY, *Bowstring.*
Knight's Move.
A Sentimental Journey: Memoirs 1917–1922.
Energy of Delusion: A Book on Plot.
Literature and Cinematography.
Theory of Prose.
Third Factory.
Zoo, or Letters Not about Love.
CLAUDE SIMON, *The Invitation.*
PIERRE SINIAC, *The Collaborators.*
JOSEF ŠKVORECKÝ, *The Engineer of Human Souls.*
GILBERT SORRENTINO,
Aberration of Starlight.
Blue Pastoral.
Crystal Vision.
Imaginative Qualities of Actual Things.
Mulligan Stew.
Pack of Lies.
Red the Fiend.
The Sky Changes.
Something Said.
Splendide-Hôtel.
Steelwork.
Under the Shadow.
W. M. SPACKMAN,
The Complete Fiction.
ANDRZEJ STASIUK, *Fado.*
GERTRUDE STEIN,
Lucy Church Amiably.
The Making of Americans.
A Novel of Thank You.
LARS SVENDSEN, *A Philosophy of Evil.*
PIOTR SZEWC, *Annihilation.*
GONÇALO M. TAVARES, *Jerusalem.*
Learning to Pray in the Age of Technology.
LUCIAN DAN TEODOROVICI,
Our Circus Presents . . .
STEFAN THEMERSON, *Hobson's Island.*
The Mystery of the Sardine.
Tom Harris.
JOHN TOOMEY, *Sleepwalker.*
JEAN-PHILIPPE TOUSSAINT,
The Bathroom.
Camera.
Monsieur.
Running Away.
Self-Portrait Abroad.
Television.
DUMITRU TSEPENEAG,
Hotel Europa.
The Necessary Marriage.
Pigeon Post.
Vain Art of the Fugue.
ESTHER TUSQUETS, *Stranded.*
DUBRAVKA UGRESIC,
Lend Me Your Character.
Thank You for Not Reading.
MATI UNT, *Brecht at Night.*
Diary of a Blood Donor.
Things in the Night.
ÁLVARO URIBE AND OLIVIA SEARS, EDS.,
Best of Contemporary Mexican Fiction.
ELOY URROZ, *Friction.*
The Obstacles.
LUISA VALENZUELA, *Dark Desires and the Others.*
He Who Searches.
MARJA-LIISA VARTIO,
The Parson's Widow.
PAUL VERHAEGHEN, *Omega Minor.*
BORIS VIAN, *Heartsnatcher.*
LLORENÇ VILLALONGA, *The Dolls' Room.*
ORNELA VORPSI, *The Country Where No One Ever Dies.*
AUSTRYN WAINHOUSE, *Hedyphagetica.*
PAUL WEST,
Words for a Deaf Daughter & Gala.
CURTIS WHITE,
America's Magic Mountain.
The Idea of Home.
Memories of My Father Watching TV.
Monstrous Possibility: An Invitation to Literary Politics.
Requiem.
DIANE WILLIAMS, *Excitability: Selected Stories.*
Romancer Erector.
DOUGLAS WOOLF, *Wall to Wall.*
Ya! & John-Juan.
JAY WRIGHT, *Polynomials and Pollen.*
The Presentable Art of Reading Absence.
PHILIP WYLIE, *Generation of Vipers.*
MARGUERITE YOUNG, *Angel in the Forest.*
Miss MacIntosh, My Darling.
REYOUNG, *Unbabbling.*
VLADO ŽABOT, *The Succubus.*
ZORAN ŽIVKOVIĆ, *Hidden Camera.*
LOUIS ZUKOFSKY, *Collected Fiction.*
SCOTT ZWIREN, *God Head.*